portuguese
whitework

Published by Vetty Creations.
PO Box 1723, Hornsby Westfield NSW 1635, Australia
Copyright © Yvette Stanton 2012.
Reprinted 2012, 2013.

www.vettycreations.com.au

Cataloguing-in-Publication data

Stanton, Yvette. 1974—
    Portuguese whitework: bullion embroidery from Guimarães

    104 p. : col. ill ; 28 cm
    Bibliography.
    Includes index.
    ISBN 9780975767757 (pbk.).

    1. Embroidery – Portugal – Guimarães Region
    2. Embroidery – Handbooks, manuals, etc.
    3. Needlework – Handbooks, manuals, etc. II. Title

746.440469

Book design: Yvette Stanton, Vetty Creations
Printed in China

other books by yvette stanton

The Left-Handed Embroiderer's Companion: a Step-by-Step Stitch Dictionary
The Right-Handed Embroiderer's Companion: a Step-by-Step Stitch Dictionary
Elegant Hardanger Embroidery
Ukrainian Drawn Thread Embroidery: Merezhka Poltavska
and with Prue Scott:
Mountmellick Embroidery: Inspired by Nature

dedication
For John.

acknowledgments
My sincere thanks go to John Stanton; Catarina Pereira, Conceição Ferreira, Isabel Oliveira, Adélia Faria of A Oficina; María Emilia Mota Prego; Patrícia Sampaio, Dr Maria Jose Meireles of Museu de Alberto Sampaio/ Instituto dos Museus e da Conservação, Guimarães; Manuel Correia (mcfotografia.com); Méri Almeida; Mary Corbet; Renee Glass; Kerrie Johnson; Prue and Tim Scott; Presencia Australia; Jeanette at Lyn's Fine Needlework; the Vetty Creations Facebook page community; readers of my blog 'White Threads'; my family.

My creativity and passion for embroidery are a gift to me from God, the source of all creativity.

Thank you to all those who have eagerly anticipated the publication of this book. Your encouragement and excitement has continually spurred me on!

selected bibliography/further reading
Fernandes, Isabel Maria. *Bordado de Guimarães: renovar a tradição/Guimarães Embroidery: a tradition renewed.* Campo das Letras, Porto, 2006.
Magalhães, M. M. de S. Calvet de. *Bordados e Rendas de Portugal.* Vega, 1995.
Moura, Maria Clementina Carneiro de. *Traditional Embroidery of Portugal.* B T Batsford Ltd, London, 1952.
Perdigão, Teresa. *Tesouros do Artesanato Português - Vol 2.* Verbo, Lisbon, 2002.
Pinto, M. H. Mendes; Klut, Ana Teresa; Museu Historico Nacional (Brazil). *Artes Tradicionais de Portugal.* Fundação Calouste Gulbenkian, Lisbon, 2004.
Sousa, António Teixeira de. *Bordados e rendas nos bragais de Entre Douro e Minho.* Programa das Artes e Ofícios Tradicionais, 1994.

photographic credits
All photos on pages 7, 8, 9 and 10:
Copyright © Manuel Correia, www.mcfotografia.com
Used by permission.
All other photos, copyright © Yvette Stanton 2012.

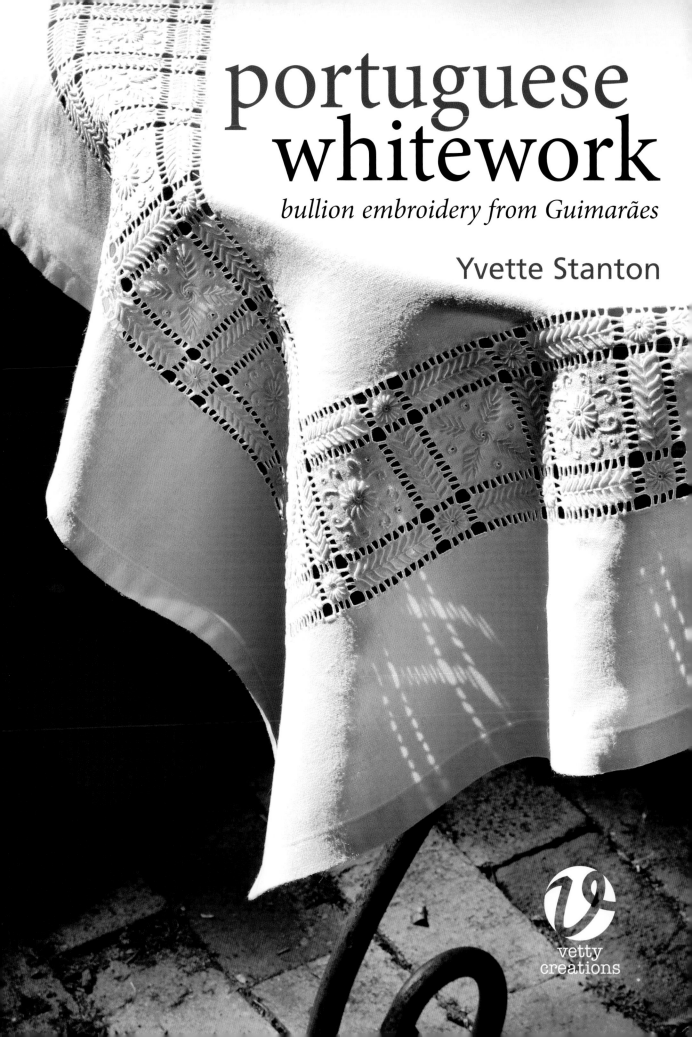

portuguese
whitework

bullion embroidery from Guimarães

Yvette Stanton

vetty
creations

contents

introduction

Some years ago I was at my embroidery guild's library, searching for any eye-catching whitework in old books. As I looked through a 1960s book on Portuguese embroidery, there was one photograph that made me immediately think, "What is that? I have to know more about that embroidery!" It was like nothing I had ever seen before: a shirt featuring gorgeous whitework, with a profusion of bullion knots combined with drawn thread work.

I learned that the embroidery I saw in the book was part of a wider style of embroidery called Guimarães embroidery, from the town of Guimarães in northern Portugal.

how to pronounce 'Guimarães'

In phonetic notation, Guimarães is written as follows: gimɐˈrẽjʃ

- g – get
- i – s<u>ee</u>
- m – al<u>m</u>ighty
- ɐ – fing<u>er</u>
- ˈ – secondary stress on following syllable
- ɾ – la<u>dd</u>er, guttural r
- ẽ – fing<u>er</u> (nasal)
- j – bo<u>y</u>
- ʃ – <u>sh</u>op

A pretty bag decorated with Guimarães embroidery, stitched and given to me by the professional embroiderers at the Oficina atelier in Guimarães.

what is Guimarães embroidery?

Guimarães embroidery is a monochrome style of embroidery, where there is the choice of only six set colours of thread: particular shades of white, black, red, blue, grey and beige. The embroidery is worked on linen, usually white or off-white. The designs are often floral, and very pretty. The embroidery is still worked in the town of Guimarães and the surrounding region, for leisure and for the tourist market.

There are two distinct styles of Guimarães embroidery. The style shown below is the more common of the two. The embroidery features stylised designs of leaves, flowers, garlands, hearts, vines. It is worked in monochrome in any of the six colours officially specified.

A hand towel from the Oficina atelier in Guimarães.

The second style of embroidery, shown below, features squares of fabric, divided by areas of drawn thread work. It is usually worked in white on white, though red, blue or black thread are less commonly used. On the squares are motifs predominantly of bullion stitch. This style is not often worked any more, as the drawn thread work is labour intensive, making the saleable work more expensive.

A hand towel worked by María Emilia Mota Prego, Guimarães, Portugal.

'Portuguese Whitework' focuses on this second style of Guimarães embroidery, the one that originally caught my eye in the old Portuguese embroidery book I found in the library.

This book explains about the history of Guimarães embroidery, the materials and equipment that are used to make it, the stitches and techniques used, and then has a wide selection of projects that feature Guimarães whitework. I have had so much joy working the embroideries in this book, and I hope that they provide you with as much enjoyment as I have had from them.

Largo da Oliveira, a large town square in the old town of Guimarães.

history

Guimarães is a town in the north of Portugal, in the Minho region, a region of rich, fertile soil, perfect for the cultivation of grapes for wine, and flax for linen. It occupies an important place in the history of Portugal as it is regarded as the birthplace of the nation. In 1139 when Alfonso Henriques declared himself King, he chose Guimarães as the capital. The old town of Guimarães is beautifully preserved, with narrow cobbled streets and ornate houses.

Guimarães embroidery is not an old style. There have been four distinct phases in the history of the embroidery. Each of these styles in turn developed to become the distinctive style of Guimarães embroidery.

phase 1 – rich embroidery

From the 1800s to the early 1900s, this earliest phase was known as *bordado rico* or rich embroidery. The work was fine, delicate and predominantly white on white. It was the embroidery found in the trousseaux of wealthy and noble young Portuguese women, and showed influences from other fine European whitework. The style was not limited to the region of Guimarães, but was widespread across the country. In 1884, The Industrial Exhibition held in Guimarães included examples of *bordado rico*, such as bedlinen and underwear. It was from this style of work that Guimarães embroidery began to develop.

phase 2 – popular embroidery

Overlapping with the end of the *bordado rico* period, from the end of 1800s to the first half 1900s, the next phase saw the popularisation of a more distinctly regional style. During this time the textile industry was becoming established in Guimarães, and cotton thread was first readily available. The new regional style of embroidery was worked on items of every day use, such as women's waistcoats and on men's workshirts.

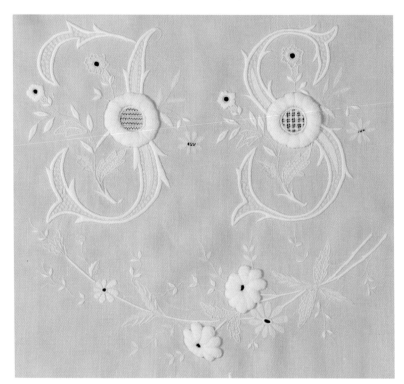

From Phase 1, face towel featuring monogram 'JS' and floral bouquet. Stitches include velvet stitch, padded satin stitch, eyelets, bullion knots. Circa 1860.
Private collection, Portugal.

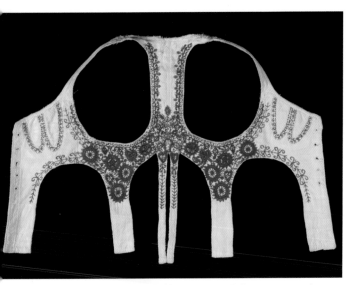

Above From Phase 2, woman's tailed waistcoat, red cotton thread on linen. Such waistcoats were worn as support garments over blouses, and were laced together at the front. Stitches include bullion, padded satin, herringbone, stem and French knots. Early 1900s.
Below Detail of waistcoat.

Collection of Museu de Alberto Sampaio, Guimarães, Portugal.

Richly embroidered, tailed linen waistcoats were worn by the women over their blouses and acted as a support garment. The embroidery was densely packed, and usually worked in red. Some waistcoats have been found worked only in black, and these would have been the garments of widows. Women's linen blouses were embroidered mainly in white.

Typically, men's linen shirts had a panel of densely packed white embroidery on the front, with a section at the base (a *ratoeira*) where the man's name was embroidered, usually in cross stitch, with red thread. These garments were worn by country folk as their best clothing for special occasions and for church attendance. They were used until they wore out, and panels of embroidery were often recycled on new garments.

phase 3 – Guimarães embroidery

Between 1940 and 1960, Guimarães embroidery began to be mentioned as a distinct style in texts. The motifs and the stitches were studied and were established along with standards for the work's execution. This sort of study was taking place across the country during this period, as people began to identify and describe various regional styles such as those from Guimarães, Viana do Castelo and Castelo Branco.

The work began to be produced in factories and rural settings, for sale. The embroidery became its own style, applied to items of everyday and special use, such as aprons, tablecloths, table mats, shirts and blouses. The embroidery became more sparse, with motifs no longer needing to fill every available inch of fabric. Instead, the embroidery may feature as a band on one end, or as a large central design.

phase 4 – renaissance of Guimarães embroidery

This phase began in the 1980s and continues until today. During this phase, the embroidery has become the subject of formal study within the region. A certification process has been devised so that the embroidery retains its unique flavour and style, and to guarantee the quality of the items that are produced for sale. All items of Guimarães embroidery that are to be sold as authentic Guimarães embroidery must be submitted for certification and approved.

This means that while the embroidery projects presented in this book fall within phase 4, strictly speaking they can only be regarded as works *in the style of* Guimarães embroidery, rather than authentic examples of Guimarães embroidery.

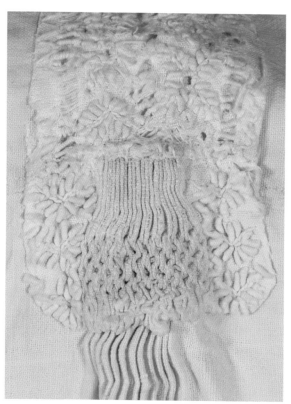

Left *From Phase 2, man's shirt, red and white cotton thread on linen. White embroidery with drawn thread work and bullion motifs. "Manoel" is stitched in red embroidery on the ratoeira. Early 1900s.*
Above *Detail of top of sleeve.*
Below *Detail of front embroidered panel*
Collection of Museu de Alberto Sampaio, Guimarães, Portugal.

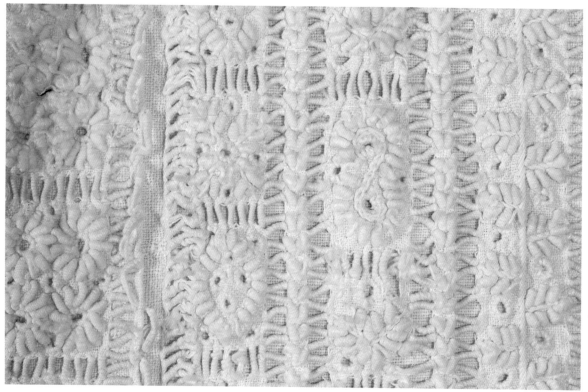

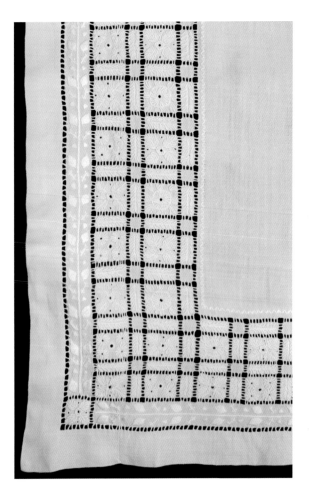

Above From Phase 4, tablecloth, white cotton on linen. This large tablecloth (approximately 2.8 x 1.6 m) features a wide border of embroidery at the edge. There is a rectangle of embroidery near the centre of the cloth, featuring similar motifs. 3rd quarter of 20th century.
Left Detail of tablecloth corner.
Below Detail of border.

Private collection, Portugal.

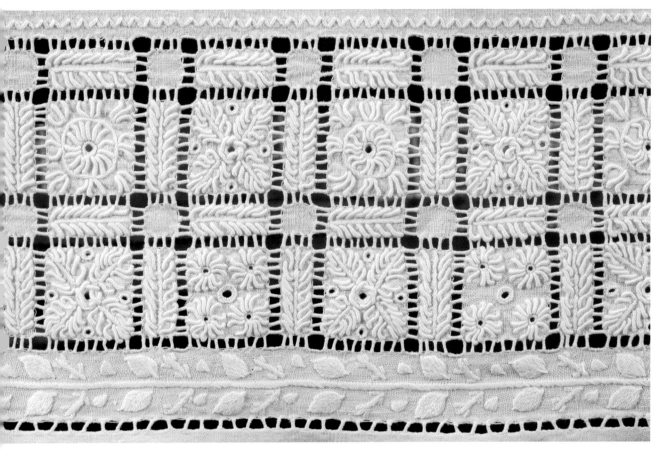

equipment and materials

In addition to general sewing supplies such as pins and embroidery scissors, you will need the following equipment and materials to make the projects in this book.

needles

Two types of needles are used for Guimarães embroidery: tapestry needles and straw needles.

Drawn thread techniques require the needle to pass cleanly between fabric threads. Tapestry needles with their blunt tips, are less likely to snag on or pierce threads. No 24 tapestry needles usually work best with pearl cotton 8. However, depending on the brand of needle, you may need a larger or smaller size as brands can vary in eye size.

Straw needles, or milliners' needles, are used for the surface stitchery. They are particularly useful for bullions as their eyes are approximately the same thickness as the shaft, so it is easier to pull them through a bullion. They are also used for the rest of the surface embroidery, as it is simpler than constantly changing needles.

Because needle sizes vary between brands, you may find that a No 3, No 4 or No 5 straw needle is best with your thread. I work primarily with No 4 straw needles.

To determine the correct size needle, the needle should be approximately the same thickness as the thread doubled over. Because the thread comes out both sides of the needle's eye, this is where it is thickest. A needle's purpose is to make a hole big enough to easily pull the thread through the fabric or wraps. If it is too thin, it is harder to pull the needle through, and leads to the thread wearing quickly. If you find that your thread is becoming very worn, change to a larger size needle.

hoops and frames

Guimarães embroiderers do not traditionally use embroidery hoops or frames, as they work with the embroidery in their hands. For those of us who are not used to producing fine, even stitching in hand, a hoop or frame helps to keep the work taut and free from puckering.

I have worked the drawn thread work both in and out of a hoop. My preference is to work without a hoop, but if I am not achieving good tension I use one. However, I always work the surface embroidery in a hoop.

magnification

The fabric used in Guimarães embroidery has a very high thread count so you may need to use magnification, particularly for accuracy with the counted tacking and the drawn thread work. In combination with magnification, good lighting such as natural light or a daylight colour lamp is essential.

marking the fabric

For drawing the motifs onto the fabric use a grey or green wash-out pencil. If wash-out pencils are unavailable, use a sharp HB pencil. I do not recommend wash-out marker pens. Whatever mark you make on the fabric will need to either be washed out or completely covered. Markings should be thin and light, rather than thick and dark. Using a lightbox or holding the fabric and pattern up to a lighted window will assist with tracing the pattern.

thread

For Guimarães embroidery in general, there are six approved DMC colours to use. Only one thread colour is used on each design – the colours are very rarely mixed. For the whitework form of Guimarães embroidery, white thread is most often used, though occasionally black, blue or red are used.

No 8 perle cotton is used exclusively. From my research, some historical examples of Guimarães embroidery appear to have been stitched in coton à broder (broder cotton), but this thread is no longer deemed as correct.

For certification of Guimarães embroidery, the official specifications include DMC colours only. While I have provided the closest Presencia and Anchor conversions for your convenience, they are by no means exact colour matches.

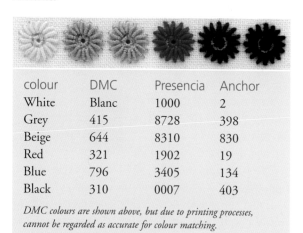

colour	DMC	Presencia	Anchor
White	Blanc	1000	2
Grey	415	8728	398
Beige	644	8310	830
Red	321	1902	19
Blue	796	3405	134
Black	310	0007	403

DMC colours are shown above, but due to printing processes, cannot be regarded as accurate for colour matching.

Different thread brands have marginally different thicknesses. While the difference can be incredibly small, it can affect the needle size. You may find that different needle sizes work better with different brands of thread.

Ensure you have enough thread for your whole project. Even for white thread, dyelots can change.

fabric

The fabric used for Guimarães whitework embroidery is 38 count linen, which is sometimes also known as 20L linen. 38 count means that there are 38 threads over a distance of one inch (2.5cm). Sometimes this may be expressed as 38tpi (threads per inch). The linen is usually white or off-white, though occasionally unbleached natural linen will be used.

Because Portuguese whitework has a counted base of drawn thread work, it is imperative that the linen be perfectly evenweave. Some people think that linen is evenweave if it does not have any 'slubs' in the threads that are often a feature of linen fabric. A fabric can be evenweave even with or without slubs. 'Evenweave' means that the thread count is the same, over the same distance, for both the warp and the weft. My survey of many different 38 count linens from around the world to test whether they are evenweave found that some are, and some are not.

For some projects, the instructions require fabric that is cut straight with the grain. This means that the fabric is carefully cut along the threads, not just anywhere across the fabric. With straight grain, the fabric will not distort as it could if it was cut across the grain.

To cut straight with the grain, either very carefully cut alongside a single thread (using good lighting!) or remove a thread and carefully cut along the gap.

determining if a fabric is evenweave

To check whether a fabric is evenweave, use the following method:

1 Insert a pin anywhere in the fabric.

2 Using a ruler or tape measure, measure 1 inch (2.5 cm) from the pin, in line with the threads of the fabric. At the end of the 1 inch (2.5cm) measurement, insert another pin into the fabric. Do this along both the warp (up and down the length of  the fabric) and the weft (left and right across the fabric, from selvedge to selvedge) from the original pin.

3 Count the threads between the original pin and the second pin. If there are 38 threads, then it has a thread count of 38. If there are 25 threads, the fabric is 25 count.

4 Count the threads between the original pin and the third pin. You will learn the thread count for the second dimension of the fabric.

If the two numbers are the same it means that the fabric is evenweave. If they are not, the fabric is not exactly evenweave. If they are only one thread different, and you are working a small project, it will be acceptable. If there is a difference of two or more threads and you are working a large project such as a tablecloth, it will not be acceptable. This is because for each inch of fabric, there are an extra two (or more) threads compared to the thread count for the other dimension. If you are working across 20 inches (50cm) there will be at least 40 extra threads. The design will work out significantly shorter in one dimension than the other, meaning a square design will not turn out square. As much as possible, the fabric you use should be exactly evenweave.

Usually thread count is measured across an inch of fabric, even in places where inches are not used as a unit of measurement. If you don't have ruler or measuring tape showing inch measurements, 2.5cm is approximately equal to 1 inch, and can be used instead.

the stitches

There are only 21 stitches that are regarded as authentic to Guimarães embroidery, and no other stitches are used in its production. While a wide variety of these stitches are used in each piece, two are seen as being the most important: *canutilho* or bullion knot, and *gradinha* or overcast bar.

the stitches of Guimarães embroidery

1 Back stitch (*atrás*)
2 Bullion knot (*canutilho*)
3 Buttonholed eyelet (*ilhó de recorte*)
4 Buttonhole stitch (*recorte*)
5 Chain stitch (*cadeia*)
6 Lazy daisy (*margarida*)
7 Double daisy (*margarida dupla*)
8 Eyelet (*ilhó de rolinho*)
9 Feather stitch (*pena simples*)
10 Fern stitch (*pé-de-galo*)
11 French knot (*nozinho*)
12 Herringbone stitch (*espinha*)
13 Overcast bar (*gradinha*)
14 Padded satin stitch (*cheio*)
15 Seed stitch (*areia*)
16 Sham hem stitch (*formiga*)
17 Stem stitch (*pé-de-flor*)
18 Whipped stem stitch (*pé-de-flor apanhado*)
19 Wide stem stitch (*pé-de-flor duplo*)
20 Straight stitch (*lançado*)
21 Velvet stitch (*veludo*)

Within the confines of the style of Guimarães embroidery on which this book focuses – whitework on a base of drawn thread work – even fewer stitches are used. These include bullion knot, buttonholed eyelet, eyelet, French knot, herringbone stitch, overcast bar, padded satin stitch, sham hem stitch, stem stitch and wide stem stitch.

portuguese whitework projects

The projects shown range from small, simple projects right through to larger and more ambitious projects. It is advisable to start with one of the simpler ones, to learn and understand the techniques, before embarking on one of the more difficult projects.

Before you begin, read through the entire project instructions and the step-by-step instructions of the listed stitches and techniques, to familiarise yourself with the whole process.

The charts for the projects are provided on two pattern sheets inserted in a pocket at the back of the book.

framed panel

This is the ideal first project, as it takes the stitcher through the entire process, introducing the basic drawn thread work techniques, and the main surface embroidery stitches used in Portuguese whitework.

difficulty 🧵
size 6 x 6 cm / 2¼ x 2¼ in
materials and equipment

- 20 x 20 cm 38 count linen, white
- 1 ball No 8 pearl cotton, white
- No 4 straw needle
- No 24 tapestry needle

chart Pattern sheet A

stitches and techniques
counted satin stitch *p48*, cutting threads *p48*, withdrawing threads *p49*, wiggly overcast bars *p57*, turning a corner *p59*, tracing patterns *p86*, bullion knot *p88*, eyelets *p90*, buttonholed eyelets *p91*, stem stitch *p96*, damp stretching *p98*

counted tacking
❶ *Very careful counting is required as this counted tacking sets up the positioning of the drawn thread work.*
1 Measure 7 cm (2¾ in) along one side from the corner of the fabric. Mark with a pin.
2 From this point, measure 7 cm (2¾ in) across the fabric. Mark with a pin.
3 Thread a needle with a long piece of pale coloured machine sewing thread.
4 Starting at the pin (which corresponds with the arrowhead on the chart), and leaving a 10 cm (4 in) tail of machine sewing thread for later use, tack parallel with the left edge of the fabric. Go under four threads, over four threads (8 threads). Go under three, over three, twelve times (72 threads). Go under four threads, over four (8 threads).
5 Turn the corner, heading along the next side of the fabric. Continuing with the same thread, repeat the tacking as for the first side.
6 Work the final two sides similarly. To finish, tack a lit-

tle further and fasten the thread with a few backstitches.
7 Rethread the long tail from the beginning of the counted tacking. Heading in the opposite direction to before, tack a little further and fasten the thread.

drawn thread work
❶ *All drawn thread work is stitched using pearl cotton and the tapestry needle. Use the counted tacking to assist with positioning.*
1 Starting with the horizontal bar at the bottom left of the chart, work the satin stitch bar. The bar has nine parallel stitches each spanning three fabric threads.
❶ *The inside edge of the bar sits on the tacking guide.*
2 Turn the corner and work the vertical satin stitch bar.
3 Leave the needle and thread ready for later use.
4 With sharp, fine-pointed scissors, cut the eight threads on the inside edge of the first nine stitches. Work slowly and carefully.
5 With the point of a needle, gently prise up one of the cut threads, close to the cut end.
6 Continue in the same way along the thread, levering it up and out, to just over halfway along the side.
7 Lever each of the other cut threads out, all the way back to the same point.
❶ *Cut them off or pin them out of the way.*
8 Returning to the working thread, bring it out at the left edge of the drawn thread area, six threads above the end of the satin stitching.
9 Working over groups of six threads, work six wiggly bars, back and forth across the drawn thread area.
❶ *Remember the anchoring stitch at the side between each bar. This stitch ensures the thread does not float across the gap between the two bars in an unsightly way.*
10 Draw back the threads in the drawn thread area up to where the next six bars will finish and the satin stitch bar will commence. Pin them out of the way.
11 Work another six wiggly bars, as before.
12 Work the satin stitch bars to turn the corner.
❶ *Do not forget the little extra stitch underneath where the first of the two satin stitch bars will be worked. This helps the end of the bar to sit correctly.*
13 Cut the eight threads at the inside edges of the bars and withdraw the threads from the first row entirely, and draw back the threads for the new row.

14 Work the wiggly bars as for the first row.

15 Continue around in the same manner to complete the square.

surface embroidery

❶ *All embroidery is worked with pearl cotton and the No 4 straw needle. If you are not already using a hoop or frame, mount the fabric in one so that it is drum tight.*

1 Trace the motif onto the centre of the fabric square inside the drawn thread work.

2 Work the centre eyelet as a regular eyelet.

3 Work the bullion stitches radiating out from the central eyelet, starting each one by bringing the needle up adjacent to the eyelet, and inserting the needle at the far end of the stitch.

4 Work the stem stitch for the 'branches', and then the bullion stitches along the sides of them.

5 Work the four outer eyelets as buttonhole eyelets.

6 Remove any tacking.

7 Damp stretch the embroidery. ❧

square mat

This pretty square mat features a ring of alternating bullion stitch motifs.

difficulty ▨▨
size 32 x 32 cm / 12¾ x 12¾ in
materials and equipment
- 40 x 40 cm (16 x 16 in) 38 count linen, white
- 2 balls No 8 pearl cotton, white
- No 4 straw needle
- No 24 tapestry needle

chart Pattern sheet B
stitches and techniques
Counted satin stitch *p48*, cutting threads *p48*, withdrawing threads *p49*, straight overcast bars *p51*, turning a corner *p53*, cross intersection *p54*, T intersection–opening end *p55*, T intersection–closing end *p56*, tracing patterns *p86*, bullion knot *p88*, eyelets *p90*, buttonholed eyelets *p91*, padded satin stitch *p94*, stem stitch *p96*, damp stretching *p98*, antique hemstitch *p100*, mitred corners *p101*

counted tacking

❶ *Very careful counting is required as this counted tacking sets up the positioning of the drawn thread work.*

1 Measure 9 cm (3½ in) along one side from the corner of the fabric. Mark with a pin.

2 From this point, measure 9 cm (3½ in) across the fabric. Mark with a pin.

3 Thread a needle with a long piece of pale coloured machine sewing thread.

4 Starting at the pin (shown by the arrowhead on the chart), and leaving a 10 cm (4 in) tail of machine sewing thread for later use, tack parallel with the left edge of the fabric. Go under four threads, over four (8 threads). Go under three, over three, twelve times (72 threads). Repeat this sequence three times. Go under four threads, over four (8 threads).

5 Turn the corner, heading along the next side of the fabric. Continuing with the same thread, repeat the tacking as for the first side.

6 Work the final two sides similarly. To finish, tack a little further and fasten the thread with a few backstitches.

7 Rethread the long tail from the beginning of the counted tacking. Heading in the opposite direction to before, tack a little further and fasten the thread.

drawn thread work

❶ *For clarity, rows have been assigned a number, and columns a letter on the Pattern Sheet. Intersections are named according to the row and column into which they fall.*

❶ *All drawn thread work is stitched using pearl cotton and the tapestry needle. Use the counted tacking to assist with positioning.*

1 Begin at the magenta arrowhead. Using the counted tacking, count eight threads to the right. Bring the needle out on the tacking line. Work the horizontal bar of nine satin stitches, positioning the bar according to the chart.

❶ *The inside edge of the bar sits on the tacking guide.*

2 Turn the corner and work the vertical satin stitch bar.

3 Leave the needle and thread hanging for later use.

4 With sharp, fine-pointed scissors, cut the eight threads on the inside edge of the first nine stitches. Work slowly and carefully.

5 With the point of a needle, gently prise up one of the cut threads, close to the cut end.

6 Continue in the same way along the thread, levering it up and out, for about 5 cm (2 in).

7 Lever each of the other cut threads out, all the way back to the same point.

❶ *Cut them off or pin them out of the way. As you work along the line of stitching, these threads will need to be withdrawn further.*

8 Returning to the working thread, bring it out at the left edge of the drawn thread area, six threads above the end of the satin stitching.

9 Work twelve straight bars from 1A to 2A. Introducing a new thread, work a 'T intersection–opening end', at 2A.

10 Work straight bars from 2A to 3A. Introducing a new thread, work a 'T intersection–opening end', at 3A.

11 Continue similarly from 3A up to 5A.

12 With the same thread, turn the corner at 5A. After working the satin stitch bars, cut the eight threads at the inside edges of the bars. Withdraw the ones from the first row entirely, and draw back the ones for the new row.

13 Work twelve bars from 5A to 5B. Introduce a new thread and work a 'T intersection–opening end' at 5B.

14 Using the newly introduced thread at 2A, work bars from 2A to 2B.

15 Using the threads at 3A and 4A, work bars from 3A to 3B and 4A to 4B.

16 Using the thread introduced at 5B, work bars from 5B to 4B, stopping one bar from the end.

17 Work a cross intersection at 4B.

18 Work bars from 4B to 3B, stopping one bar from the end of the section.

19 Picking up the thread from 3A–3B, lace it behind the final bar of 4B–3B. Work the final bar of 4B–3B, wrapping the laced thread along with the fabric threads.

20 Using the same thread, work a satin stitch bar. Cut and withdraw the threads at the inside edge.

21 Finish off the laced thread by running it under the back of the satin stitch bar. Trim any excess.

22 Picking up the thread from 4B–3B, continue on, working bars from 3B to 2B, stopping one bar from the end of the section.

23 Work a cross intersection at 2B, then work bars from 2B to 1B.

24 Picking up the thread at 5B, work bars from 5B to 5C. Introducing a new thread, work a 'T intersection–opening end' at 5C.

25 Work bars from 5C to 5D. Work a 'T intersection–opening end' at 5D to start a new thread.

26 Work bars from 5D to 5E. Work the corner satin stitch bars. Cut and withdraw the threads. Work bars from 5E to 4E, stopping one bar from the end.

27 Picking up the thread at 5C, work bars from 5C to 4C.

28 Picking up the thread at 4B, work bars from 4B to 4C. Work a 'T intersection–closing end' to finish off the thread coming across from 5C.

29 Picking up the thread at 5D, work bars from 5D to 4D, stopping one bar from the end.

30 Picking up the thread at 4C, work bars from 4C to 4D. Work a cross intersection at 4D.

31 Continuing with the same thread, work the bars from 4D to 4E. Lace the thread behind the final bar of the 5E to 4E section.

32 Work the final bar of 5E to 4E, including the laced thread. Work the satin stitch bar at 4E. Cut and withdraw the threads at the inside edge of the satin stitch bar.

33 Finish off the laced thread by running it under the back of the satin stitch bar. Trim any excess.

34 Continuing with the thread from the satin stitch bar, work bars from 4E to 3E. Introducing a new thread, work a 'T intersection–opening end' at 3E.

35 With the new thread, work bars from 3E to 3D.

36 Picking up the thread at 4D, work bars from 4D to 3D. Work a 'T intersection–closing end' to finish off the 3E–3D thread.

37 Work bars from 3D to 2D, stopping one from the end.

38 Picking up the thread at 3E, work bars from 3E to 2E, stopping one bar from the end.

39 Pick up the thread at 2B and work bars from 2B to 2C. Work a 'T intersection–opening end' at 2C.

40 Work bars from 2C to 2D.

41 Work a cross intersection at 2D.

42 Work bars from 2D to 2E. Lace the thread behind the final bar of the 3E to 2E section.

43 Work the final bar of 3E to 2E, wrapping the laced thread along with the fabric threads.

44 Using the same thread, work a satin stitch bar. Cut and withdraw the threads at the inside edge.

45 Finish off the laced thread by running it under the back of the satin stitch bar. Trim any excess.

46 Continuing on with the 3E–2E thread, work bars from 2E to 1E. Turn the corner with satin stitch bars. Cut and withdraw the threads as required.

47 Work bars from 1E to 1D, stopping one from the end.

48 Pick up the thread at 2D and work bars from 2D to 1D. Lace the thread behind the final bar of 1E–1D.

49 Work the final bar of 1E to 1D, wrapping the laced thread along with the fabric threads.

50 Using the same thread, work a satin stitch bar. Cut and withdraw the threads at the inside edge.

51 Finish off the laced thread by running it under the back of the satin stitch bar. Trim any excess.

52 Continuing on with the 1E–1D thread, work bars from 1D to 1C, stopping one bar from the end.

53 Pick up the thread at 2C and work bars from 2C to 1C. Lace the thread behind the final bar of the 1D–1C.

54 Work the final bar of 1D to 1C, wrapping the laced thread along with the fabric threads.

55 Using the same thread, work a satin stitch bar. Cut and withdraw the threads at the inside edge.

56 Finish off the laced thread by running it under the back of the satin stitch bar. Trim any excess.

57 Continuing on with the 1D–1C thread, work bars from 1C to 1B, stopping one bar from the end.

58 Picking up the 2B–1B thread, lace it behind the final bar of 1C–1B.

59 Work the final bar of 1C to 1B, wrapping the laced thread along with the fabric threads.

60 Using the same thread, work a satin stitch bar. Cut and withdraw the threads at the inside edge.

61 Finish off the laced thread by running it under the back of the satin stitch bar. Trim any excess.

62 Continuing on with the 1C–1B thread, work bars from 1B to 1A. Finish the thread by running it under the back of the satin stitch bar. Trim any excess.

surface embroidery

❶ *All embroidery is worked with pearl cotton and the No 4 straw needle. If you are not already using a hoop or frame, mount the fabric in one so that it is drum tight.*

1 Using the chart, trace the motifs onto the centre of each drawn thread work fabric square.

2 'Leaves' motifs: Work the centre circle in padded satin stitch. Stitch the curved bullions around the centre. Work the stem stitch stems. Work bullion stitch leaves down the stems. Stitch the eyelets at the middle of each side.

3 'Flower' motifs: Work five buttonholed eyelets; a larger central one, and four smaller ones towards the corners. Work bullion stitches radiating out from each corner eyelet. Start each bullion by bringing the needle up next to the eyelet, taking the needle down at the stitch's far end.

finishing

1 Measure out 4.5 cm (1¾ in) from the edge of the drawn thread area on each side of the fabric. Run a line of tacking around the fabric at this measurement. Ensure the tacking completely aligns with the fabric grain.

2 Measure out 7.5 cm (3 in) from the edge of the drawn thread area on each side of the fabric and carefully trim at this measurement, along the grain of the fabric.

3 Work mitred corners, folding in 1 cm (⅜ in) each time.

4 Pin or tack the hems in place.

5 Just inside the tacked line, cut a single thread at the centre of each side and draw it back to the corners of that side. Bury the ends within the hem.

6 Using antique hemstitch and grouping the threads together in groups of four, hemstitch the hems.

❶ *Towards the end of each side, you may find that the number of threads is not divisible by four. If this is the case, work one or two groups of three e.g. if there are 14 threads remaining, work two groups of four, then two groups of three.*

7 Remove all tacking. Damp stretch the embroidery. ✿

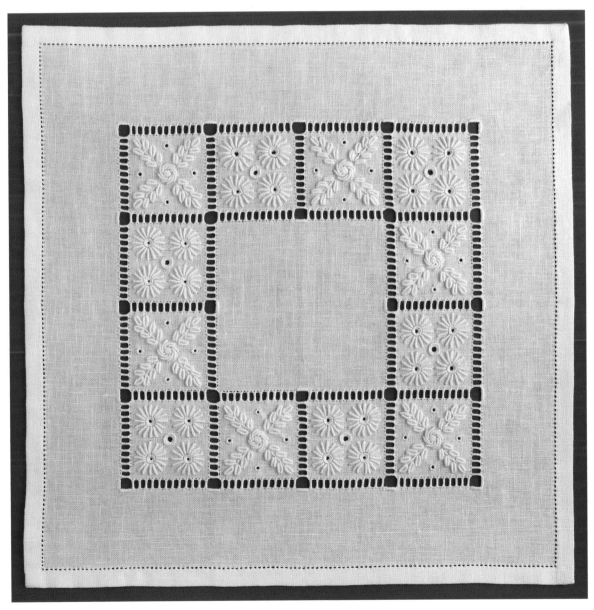

biscornu

A biscornu is an eight-pointed pillow often used as a pin-cushion.

difficulty 🔳🔳

size 11 x 11 x 4 cm / 4¼ x 4¼ x 1½ in

materials and equipment

- 30 x 30 cm (12 x 12 in) 38 count linen, white
- 1 ball No 8 pearl cotton, white
- No 24 tapestry needle
- No 4 straw needle
- 2 buttons, 15 mm (1⅝ in) diameter, 1 for top, 1 for base
- 1 piece patchwork fabric, 13.5 x 13.5 cm (5¼ x 5¼ in) to line the embroidered panel
- 1 piece patchwork fabric, 13.5 x 13.5 cm (5¼ x 5¼ in) for the base of the biscornu
- polyester fibre fill

chart Pattern sheet A

stitches and techniques

counted satin stitch *p48*, cutting threads *p48*, withdrawing threads *p49*, straight overcast bars *p51*, turning a corner *p53*, cross intersection *p54*, T intersection – opening end *p55*, T intersection – closing end *p56*, tracing patterns *p86*, bullion knot *p88*, eyelets *p90*, buttonholed eyelets *p91*, stem stitch *p96*, damp stretching *p98*, ladder stitch *p103*

counted tacking

❶ *Very careful counting is required as this counted tacking sets up the positioning of the drawn thread work.*

1 Measure 10.5 cm (4 in) along one side from the corner of the fabric. Mark with a pin.

2 From this point, measure 10.5 cm (4 in) across the fabric. Mark with a pin.

3 Thread a needle with a long piece of pale coloured machine sewing thread.

4 Starting at the pin (which corresponds with the arrowhead on the chart), and leaving a 10 cm (4 in) tail of machine sewing thread for later use, tack parallel with the left edge of the fabric. Go under four threads, over four threads (8 threads). Go under three threads, over three threads, four times (24 threads). Go under four threads, over four (8 threads). Go under three, over three threads, ten times (60 threads). Go under four threads, over four (8 threads). Go under three, over three threads, four times (24 threads). Go under four threads, over four (8 threads).

5 Turn the corner, heading along the next side of the fabric. Continuing with the same thread, repeat the tacking as for the first side.

6 Work the final two sides in the same way. To finish, tack a little further and fasten the thread.

7 Rethread the long tail from the beginning of the counted tacking. Heading in the opposite direction to before, tack a little further and fasten the thread.

drawn thread work

❶ *For clarity, rows have been assigned a number, and columns a letter on the Pattern Sheet. Intersections are named according to the row and column into which they fall.*

❶ *All drawn thread work is stitched using pearl cotton and the tapestry needle. Use the counted tacking to assist with positioning.*

1 Beginning at the magenta arrowhead and using the counted tacking, count eight threads to the right. Bring the needle out on the tacking line. Work the horizontal bar of nine satin stitches, positioning the bar according to the chart.

❶ *The inside edge of the bar sits on the tacking guide.*

2 Turn the corner and work the vertical satin stitch bar.

3 Leave the needle and thread ready for later use.

4 With sharp, fine-pointed scissors, cut the eight threads on the inside edge of each of the two satin stitch bars. Work slowly and carefully.

5 With the point of a needle, gently prise up one of the ends of the cut threads next to the first satin stitch bar.

6 Continue in the same way along the thread, levering it up and out, for about 5 cm (2 in).

7 Lever each of the cut threads out to the same place.

❶ *Cut them off or pin them out of the way. As you work along the line, the threads will need to be withdrawn further.*

8 Run a new thread underneath the satin stitching and lace it behind the threads to be wrapped in the first bar.

9 Returning to the working thread, bring it out at the left edge of the drawn thread area, six threads above the end of the satin stitching.

10 Work four straight bars from 1A to 2A, wrapping the laced thread along with the fabric threads in the first bar. Work a 'T-intersection–opening end' at 2A.

11 Work a total of ten bars from 2A to 3A. Introducing a new thread, work a 'T intersection–opening end' at 3A.

12 Work a total of four straight bars from 3A to 4A. Turn the corner with satin stitch bars. Cut and withdraw threads as required.

13 Picking up the thread at 1A, work bars from 1A to 1B.

14 Picking up the threads at 2A, 3A and 4A, work four bars from 2A to 2B, 3A to 3B and 4A to 4B respectively.

15 Work a 'T intersection–opening end' at 4B. Work bars from 4B to 3B, stopping one bar from the end.

16 Work a cross intersection at 3B, then work bars from 3B to 2B, stopping one bar from the end.

17 Work a cross intersection at 2B, then work four bars from 2B to 1B.

18 Work a 'T intersection – closing end' at 1B. Work bars from 1B to 1C, stopping one bar from the end.
19 Picking up the threads at 2B, 3B and 4B, work bars from 2B to 2C, 3B to 3C and 4B to 4C respectively.
20 Work a 'T intersection – opening end' at 4C. Work bars from 4C to 3C, stopping one bar from the end.
21 Work a cross intersection at 3C, then the bars from 3C to 2C, stopping one bar from the end.
22 Work a cross intersection at 2B, then the bars from 2C to 1C.
23 Work a 'T intersection – closing end' at 1C. Continue, working bars from 1C to 1D.
24 Picking up the threads at 2C, 3C and 4C, work bars from 2C to 2D, 3C to 3D and 4C to 4D respectively.
25 Lace the threads at 2D and 3D behind the adjacent bars in column D.

26 Picking up the thread at 4D, work the corner with satin stitch bars. Cut and withdraw the threads as required.
27 Work three bars from 4D to 3D. Work the fourth bar, including the laced thread with the fabric threads.
28 Work a satin stitch bar at 3D. Cut and withdraw the threads at the inside edge. Finish off the laced thread by running it through the back of the satin stitch. Trim the thread.
29 Work bars from 3D to 2D. Work the last bar including the laced thread with the fabric threads.
30 Work a satin stitch bar at 2D. Cut and withdraw the threads at the inside edge. Finish off the laced thread by running it through the back of the satin stitch. Trim the thread.
31 Work four bars from 2D to 1D. Work the corner with satin stitch bars. Cut and withdraw threads as needed. Finish off both remaining working threads by running them through the back of the satin stitch.

surface embroidery

❶ *All embroidery is worked with pearl cotton and the No 4 straw needle. If you are not already using a hoop or frame, mount the fabric in one so that it is drum tight.*

1 Using the chart, trace the motifs onto the centre of each drawn thread work fabric square and rectangle.

2 Work eyelets in the corner squares. Work bullion stitches radiating out from the eyelet. Start each one by bringing the needle up adjacent to the eyelet, taking the needle to the back at the far end of the stitch.

3 Work the stem stitch 'veins' along the centre of the rectangular panels. Work the bullion 'leaves' down each side.

4 Stitch the bullions radiating out from the centre of the centre square. Work buttonhole eyelets at the corners.

construction

1 Remove the tacking. Damp stretch the embroidery.

2 With the embroidery centred, trim the linen to 13.5 cm (5¼ in) square.

3 Place the embroidered panel face up on top of the patchwork fabric lining square. Pin, then baste the two fabrics together. On the back of each piece of patchwork fabric, draw a line 1 cm (⅜ in) from each edge. This will be the stitching line. Mark the midpoint of each line.

4 At the middle of each side carefully cut just over halfway into the seam allowance.

❶ *If you cut too far, it will lead to weak and messy corners.*

5 With the right sides of the fabric together, align one seamline corner of the linen/patchwork panel with the midpoint of the base piece. Align the raw edges, so that the upper fabric's midpoint on the same side aligns with the seamline corner of the base piece.

6 With matching thread, and starting right at the seamline corner (do not sew within the seam allowance), machine stitch to the midpoint exactly. Take the fabric out of the sewing machine. Finish the thread ends.

❶ *White thread is shown for illustration purposes only.*

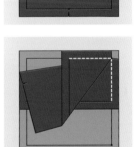

7 Realign the fabric edges so that the next seamline corner of the top fabric aligns with the midpoint of the base fabric. Pin to hold it in place. Start stitching where you left off, down the newly aligned sides. Stop exactly at the seamline corner. Take the fabric out of the sewing machine. Finish the thread ends.

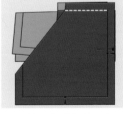

8 Realign the fabric edges so that the next midpoint of the upper fabric aligns with the seamline corner of the base fabric. Starting anew at the end of the previous sewing, continue stitching.

9 Continue in the same way, around each side, leaving a gap of about 4 cm (1⅝ in) in the final side. Cease stitching and tie off the ends of the threads.

10 Turn the biscornu right side out, pushing the corners out as far as they will go, to make crisp corners.

11 Fill the biscornu with fibre fill, so that it is well stuffed. Ladder stitch the last side closed.

12 Align the middle of the top of the biscornu as closely as possible with the middle of the base. Using a doubled machine sewing thread, securely stitch from the top through to the base a few times, tightening the stitches a little to make a 'dimple'.

13 With a matching thread, stitch the top button in the space at the middle of the top of the biscornu.

14 With a matching thread, stitch the button for the base securely in place. ✆

hanging ornaments

Even though they are not a traditional application of Guimarães embroidery, these pretty little ornaments would enhance any Christmas tree. They make wonderful gifts, being small and relatively quick to create.

difficulty ▤

size 10 x 20 cm / 4 x 8 in incl. hanging loop and bell

materials and equipment

- 1 ball No 8 pearl cotton, DMC 310 (black), DMC 321 (red), DMC 415 (grey), DMC 644 (beige), DMC 796 (blue), 1 colour per ornament
- 15 x 15 cm (6 x 6 in) 38 count linen, white, per ornament
- 2 squares patchwork fabric in co-ordinating colours, 10 x 10 cm (4 x 4 in), per ornament
- 2 squares 1 mm (¹⁄₃₂ in) thick cardboard, 7 x 7 cm (2¾ x 2¾ in) per ornament
- 2 squares felt, 7 x 7 cm (2¾ x 2¾ in) per ornament
- small gold or silver coloured bell, per ornament
- 30 cm (12 in) white ribbon, 4 mm (⅛ in) wide, per ornament
- 30 cm (12 in) mini ric-rac, per ornament
- No 4 straw needle
- No 24 tapestry needle
- No 9 embroidery needle
- white machine sewing thread
- glue stick

charts Pattern sheet B

stitches and techniques

counted satin stitch *p48*, cutting threads *p48*, withdrawing threads *p49*, straight overcast bars *p51*, turning a corner *p53*, tracing patterns *p86*, bullion knot *p88*, eyelets *p90*, buttonholed eyelets *p91*, French knot *p92*, stem stitch *p96*, lacing fabric *p102*, ladder stitch *p103*

counted tacking

❶ *Very careful counting is required as this counted tacking sets up the positioning of the drawn thread work.*

1 Measure 5 cm (2 in) along one side from the corner of the fabric. Mark with a pin.

2 From this point, measure 5 cm (2 in) across the fabric. Mark with a pin.

3 Starting at the pin (which corresponds with the arrowhead on the chart), and leaving a 10 cm (4 in) tail of machine sewing thread for later use, tack parallel with the left edge of the fabric. Go under four threads, over four threads (8 threads). Go under three, over three, ten times (60 threads). Finish the side by going under four threads, over four (8 threads).

4 Turn the corner, heading along the next side of the fabric. Continuing with the same thread, repeat the tacking as for the first side.

5 Work the final two sides in the same way. To finish, tack a little further and fasten the thread.

6 Rethread the long tail from the beginning of the counted tacking. Heading in the opposite direction to before, tack a little further and fasten the thread.

drawn thread work

❶ *All drawn thread work is stitched using pearl cotton and the tapestry needle. Use the counted tacking to assist with positioning.*

1 Begin at the magenta arrowhead. Use the counted tacking to count eight threads to the right. Bring the needle out on the tacking line. Work the horizontal bar of nine satin stitches, positioning the bar according to the chart.

❶ *The inside edge of the bar sits on the tacking guide.*

2 Turn the corner and work the vertical satin stitch bar.

3 Leave the needle and thread ready for later use.

4 With sharp, fine-pointed scissors, cut the eight threads on the inside edge of the first nine stitches. Work slowly and carefully.

5 With the point of a needle, gently prise up one of the cut threads, close to the cut end.

6 Continue in the same way along the thread, levering it up and out, to just past the centre of the side.

7 Lever each of the other cut threads out, all the way back to the same point.

❶ *Cut them off or pin them out of the way.*

8 Returning with the working thread, bring it out at the right edge of the drawn thread area, six threads above the end of the satin stitching.

9 Working over groups of six threads work five straight bars.

10 Draw back the threads in the drawn thread area up to where the next five bars will finish and the satin stitch bar will commence. Pin them out of the way.

11 Work five more straight bars, as before.

12 Work the satin stitch bars to turn the corner.

❶ *Do not forget the little extra stitch underneath where the satin stitch bar will be worked. This helps the end of the bar to sit correctly.*

13 On completion of both satin stitch bars, cut the eight threads at the inside edges of the bars and withdraw the ones from the first row entirely, and draw back the ones for the new row.

14 Work the straight bars as for the first row.

15 Continue around, to complete the square.

surface embroidery

❶ *All embroidery is worked with pearl cotton and the No 4 straw needle. If you are not already using a hoop or frame, mount the fabric in one so that it is drum tight.*

❶ *Work each coloured square according to its chart.*

1 Trace the motif onto the centre of the fabric square inside the drawn thread work.

2 Work all eyelets and buttonhole eyelets first.

3 On the grey square, work the stem stitch ring. On the beige square, work the stem stitch hearts.

4 On the beige square work the French knots (with one wrap each) in the hearts.

5 Work the bullion stitches.

finishing

1 Remove the tacking. Measure out 2.5 cm (1 in) from the edge of the drawn thread area on each side, and mark. Trim across at this point, creating a trimmed embroidery panel of 10 x 10 cm (4 x 4 in).

2 With a small dab of the glue stick, attach the felt to the cardboard, to stop the felt moving during construction. Repeat for the other felt and cardboard squares.

❶ *You will need two for each ornament.*

3 Lay the backing fabric over the felt side of one of the squares of cardboard. With a very long, doubled piece of machine sewing thread in the embroidery needle, tightly lace back and forth across two opposite sides. Finish with a back stitch or two to fasten the thread.

4 Check that the embroidery is centred on the front. If it is not, adjust it. Turn the work and lace the other two sides.

5 Place the embroidered panel right side up over the front of the lining fabric. Working with them sandwiched together, lay them over the felt side of one of the cardboard squares. Using doubled machine sewing thread, lace the front panel.

6 Lay the ric-rac along one side of the back of the front panel, so that half of the ric-rac extends over the edge. Using a matching thread colour, carefully sew the ric-rac in place along the edge of each side. Ease extra into the corners. Bend the raw ends in and stitch them in place, so they will be neatly covered when the front and back panels are sewn together.

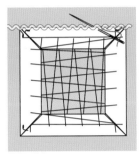

❶ *Contrasting thread shown for illustration purposes only.*

7 Cut a piece of ribbon 20 cm (8 in) long. Fold the ribbon in half and bring the ends together. Stitch the ends together 1 cm (⅜ in) in from the raw ends. Sew this securely to the back of the front panel at the top so that the folded ribbon forms the hanging loop.

8 Place the front and back panels together, with wrong sides in. Starting at the top, ladder stitch along the edges, stitching through the ric-rac where it sits out from the edge, as needed. Stitch down to the bottom of the ornament (opposite the hanging loop).

9 With 10 cm (4 in) ribbon, thread one end through the hanging loop of one of the bells. Tie the ribbon into a small, neat bow.

10 Neatly and securely sew the bow onto the bottom of the ornament, and continue ladder stitching up the remaining two sides of the ornament. Finish the thread neatly and securely on the back. ❧

table runner

This pretty table runner will make an elegant addition to any table or sideboard. If you prefer, it could easily be made into a bell pull by hemming a long pocket into the top and bottom ends in which to insert bell pull rods.

difficulty ▮▮▮

size 43 x 19 cm / 16¾ x 7⅜ in

materials and equipment

- 50 x 25 cm (20 x 10 in) 38 count linen, white
- 2 balls No 8 pearl cotton, white
- No 24 tapestry needle
- No 4 straw needle

chart Pattern sheet A

stitches and techniques

counted satin stitch *p48*; cutting threads *p48*; withdrawing threads *p49*; wiggly overcast bars *p57*; turning a corner *p59*; T intersection–opening end M3 *p64*, ME *p65*; T intersection–closing end M3 *p66*, ME *p67*; T bar intersection–opening end SW *p70*, ZM *p71*; T bar intersection–closing end MS *p72*, WZ *p73*; tracing patterns *p86*; bullion knot *p88*; eyelets *p90*; buttonholed eyelets *p91*; stem stitch *p96*; damp stretching *p98*; antique hemstitch *p100*; mitred corners *p101*

counted tacking

❶ *Very careful counting is required as this counted tacking sets up the positioning of the drawn thread work.*

1 Measure 8 cm (3¼ in) along one side from the corner of the fabric. Mark with a pin.

2 From this point, measure 8 cm (3¼ in) across the fabric. Mark with a pin.

3 Thread a needle with a long piece of pale coloured machine sewing thread.

4 Starting at the pin (which corresponds with the arrowhead on the chart), and leaving a 10 cm (4 in) tail of machine sewing thread for later use, tack parallel with the bottom edge of the fabric. Go under four threads, over four threads (8 threads). Go under three and over three threads, four times (24 threads). Go under four threads, over four threads (8 threads). Go under two threads (2 threads). Go over three threads, under three threads, nine times (54 threads). Go over two threads (2 threads). Go under four threads, over four threads (8 threads). Go under three and over three threads, four times (24 threads). Go under four threads, over four threads (8 threads).

5 Turn the corner, heading along the next side of the fabric. Continuing with the same thread, go under four threads, over four threads (8 threads). Go under two threads

(2 threads). Go over three threads, under three threads, 83 times (498 threads). Go over two threads (2 threads). Go under four threads, over four threads (8 threads).

6 Turn the corner. Repeat the tacking for the first side.

7 Turn the corner and repeat the tacking for the second side. To finish, tack a little further and fasten the thread.

8 Rethread the long tail from the beginning of the counted tacking. Heading in the opposite direction to before, tack a little further and fasten the thread.

9 With a new thread, begin a new line of tacking with a few backstitches just below the right edge of 1B intersection. Heading towards the far end of the runner, insert the needle on the first tacked line and go under four threads, over four threads (8 threads). Go under two

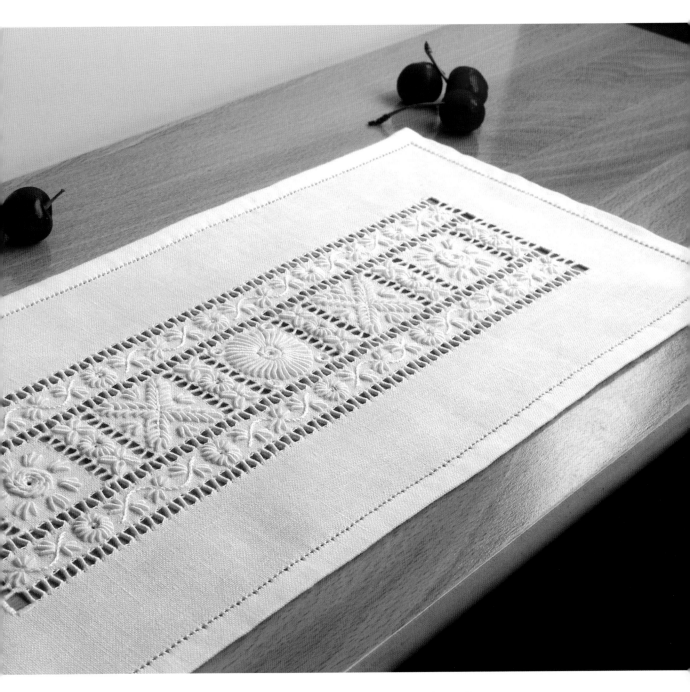

threads (2 threads). Go over three threads, under three threads, three times (18 threads). Go over two threads (2 threads). Go under four threads, over four threads (8 threads). Go under two threads (2 threads). Go over three threads, under three threads, nine times (54 threads). Go over two threads (2 threads). Repeat this sequence four more times. Go under four threads, over four threads (8 threads). Go under two threads (2 threads). Go over three threads, under three threads, three times (18 threads). Go over two threads (2 threads). Go under four threads, over four threads (8 threads). Tack a little further and fasten the thread.

10 Repeat this tacking starting to the left side of 1C intersection, heading towards the far end of the runner.

drawn thread work

❶ *For clarity, rows have been assigned a number, and columns a letter on the Pattern Sheet. Intersections are named according to the row and column into which they fall.*

❶ *All drawn thread work is stitched using pearl cotton and the tapestry needle. Use the counted tacking to assist with positioning.*

1 Begin at the magenta arrowhead (1D) and using the counted tacking, count eight threads up. Bring the needle out on the tacking line. Work the vertical bar of nine satin stitches, positioning the bar according to the chart.

❶ *The inside edge of the bar sits on the tacking guide.*

2 Turn the corner. Work the horizontal satin stitch bar.

3 Leave the needle and thread hanging for later use.

27

4 With sharp, fine-pointed scissors, cut the eight threads on the inside edge of each of the two satin stitch bars. Work slowly and carefully.

5 With the point of a needle, gently prise up one of the ends of the cut threads next to the first satin stitch bar.

6 Continue in the same way along the thread, levering it up and out, for about 5 cm (2 in).

7 Lever each of the cut threads out to the same place.

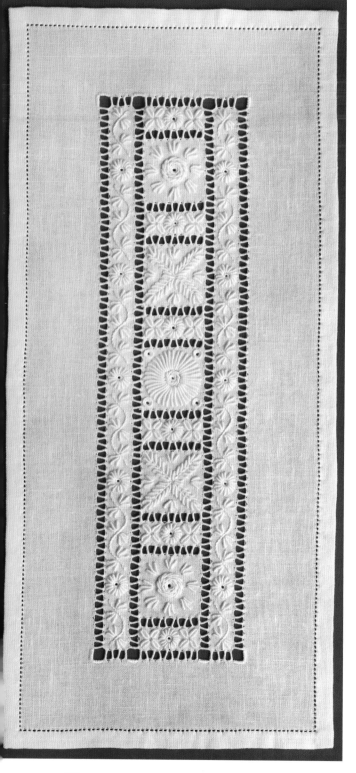

❶ *Cut them off or pin them out of the way. As you work along the line, the threads will need to be withdrawn further.*

8 Bring the thread out at the edge of the drawn thread area, six threads along from the end of the satin stitching.

9 Heading from 1D to 1C, work four wiggly bars.

10 Introducing a new thread, work a 'T intersection – opening end M3'. As part of the T intersection, the first bar of 1C to 1B is worked over only five threads.

❶ *In this project, some bars are worked over only five threads at the ends of rows, rather than the usual six threads.*

11 Continue from 1C to 1B, working eight wiggly bars over six threads as usual, stopping one bar from the end.

12 Work the last bar of 1C to 1B over five threads only. At the same time, introducing a new thread, work a 'T intersection – opening end ME'.

13 Continuing with the same thread as before, work four wiggly bars from 1B to 1A.

14 Turn the corner at 1A, cutting and withdrawing threads as needed.

15 Heading towards 12A, work the first wiggly bar over only five threads. Continuing on, work 82 wiggly bars over groupings of six threads. Finish the row with a wiggly bar over five threads.

16 At 12A, turn the corner with satin stitch bars, and finish the thread by running it under the back of the satin stitching. Trim the thread. Cut and withdraw fabric threads as required.

17 Pick up the thread at 1B and work the first bar heading towards 2B over five bars only. Work the next four wiggly bar over six threads as usual.

18 At 2B, work a 'T bar intersection – opening end SW' to start the new row with a new thread.

❶ *The first bar in each new row is worked over only five threads. The last bar in each of these rows is also worked over only five threads.*

19 Continuing on with the same thread as before, work eight wiggly bars from 2B to 3B, stopping one bar before where the intersection will be.

20 Introducing a new thread, work a 'T bar intersection – opening end ZM' at 3B.

21 Continue up the B column, working wiggly bars over groups of six threads. At 4B, work a 'T bar intersection – opening end SW'. At 5B, work a 'T bar intersection – opening end ZM'. At 6B, work a 'T bar intersection – opening end SW'. At 7B, work a 'T bar intersection – opening end ZM'. At 8B, work a 'T bar intersection – opening end SW'. At 9B, work a 'T bar intersection – opening end ZM'. At 10B, work a 'T bar intersection – opening end SW'. At 11B, work a 'T bar intersection – opening end ZM'.

22 Work two more wiggly bars over six threads, stopping one bar before the 12B intersection. Work the final bar over five threads only.

23 Picking up each of the threads at 2B, 3B, 4B etc,

right up to 11B, work across the rows, stopping one bar before each row ends at C.

24 Pick up the thread at 1C and work the first bar heading towards 2C over five bars only. Work the next four wiggly bars over six threads each as usual.

25 At 2C, work a 'T bar intersection – closing end WZ' to complete the 2B-2C row.

❶ *Work the last bar in each of these rows over only five threads.*

26 Continue up the C column, working wiggly bars over groups of six threads. At 3C, work a 'T bar intersection – closing end MS'. At 4C, work a 'T bar intersection – closing end WZ'. At 5C, work a 'T bar intersection – closing end MS'. At 6C, work a 'T bar intersection – closing end WZ'. At 7C, work a 'T bar intersection – closing end MS'. At 8C, work a 'T bar intersection – closing end WZ'. At 9C, work a 'T bar intersection – closing end MS'. At 10C, work a 'T bar intersection – closing end WZ'. At 11C, work a 'T bar intersection – closing end MS'.

27 Work two more wiggly bars over six threads, stopping one bar before the 12C intersection. Work the final bar over five threads only.

28 Start a new thread by running it under the back of the satin stitch at 1D. Heading towards 12D, work the first wiggly bar over only five threads. Continuing on, work 82 wiggly bars over groupings of six threads. Finish the row with a wiggly bar over five threads.

29 At 12D, turn the corner with satin stitch bars. Cut and withdraw threads as required.

30 Heading from 12D to 12C, work four wiggly bars.

31 At 12C, work a 'T intersection – closing end ME', with the first bar of the 12C-12B section worked over only five threads.

32 Work eight more bars over six thread groupings towards 12B, stopping one bar before the end.

33 At 12B, work a 'T intersection – closing end M3', with the final bar of 12C-12B worked over only five threads.

34 From 12B to 12A work four wiggly bars. Finish the thread by running it under the back of the satin stitching. Trim the thread.

35 Remove the tacking.

surface embroidery

❶ *All embroidery is worked with pearl cotton and the No 4 straw needle. If you are not already using a hoop or frame, mount the fabric in one so that it is drum tight.*

1 Using the chart, centre and trace the motifs onto each drawn thread work fabric square and rectangle.

2 For the side borders work all the stem stitch first, followed by the bullions along their sides. Work the eyelets and then the bullions radiating out from them.

3 For the short rectangular panels, work the eyelets and then the bullions radiating out from them. Work the leaves in bullion stitch.

4 For the top and bottom squares, work a buttonhole eyelet in the centre. Work the bullions curling around, and then the outer groups of bullions.

5 For the centre square, work the buttonhole stitch eyelets. Work bullions curling around the centre eyelet. Work long, radiating bullions around this.

6 Work the stem stitch in the remaining squares. Work the bullion stitch 'leaves' down each side of the stem stitch. Stitch the remaining bullions between the stems.

finishing

1 Damp stretch the embroidery.

2 Measure out 4 cm (1½ in) from the edge of the drawn thread area on each side of the fabric and run a line of tacking around at this point. Ensure the tacking is straight with the grain.

3 Measure out 7 cm (2¾ in) from the edge of the drawn thread area on each side of the fabric and trim along the grain of the fabric.

4 Work mitred corners, folding in 1 cm (⅜ in) each time.

5 Pin or tack the hems in place.

6 Just inside the tacked line, cut a single thread at the centre of each side and draw it back to the corners of that side. Bury the ends within the hem.

7 Using antique hemstitch and grouping the threads together in groups of four, hemstitch the hems.

❶ *Towards the end of each side, you may find the number of threads is not divisible by four. If this is the case, work one or two groups of three e.g. if there are 14 threads remaining, work two groups of four, then two groups of three.*

8 Remove the tacking. ❧

tablecloth

This elegant tablecloth with its extravagant embroidered border will make a stunning focal point on any table.

difficulty ▰▰▱

size   100 x 100 cm / 39½ x 39½ in

materials and equipment

- 108 x 108 cm (42½ x 42½ in) 38 count linen, white, cut straight with the grain of the fabric
- 8 balls No 8 pearl cotton, white
- No 24 tapestry needle
- No 4 straw needle
- Pale coloured machine-sewing thread for tacking, white for hems

Note on fabric: you will need to ensure that the fabric is definitely evenweave fabric (the same thread count across both the width and length of the fabric, over the same distance) as if it is not, it will be very obvious over such long spans, with the embroidery turning out rectangular rather than square.

charts   Part A on Pattern sheet A, part B on Pattern sheet B, full mini pattern on Pattern sheet A

stitches and techniques

counted satin stitch *p48*; cutting threads *p48*; withdrawing threads *p49*; wiggly overcast bars *p57*; turning a corner *p59*, cross intersection M3 *p60*, W3 *p62*; T intersection – opening end M3 *p64*, ME *p65*; T intersection – closing end W3 *p68*, WE *p69*; tracing patterns *p86*; bullion knot *p88*; eyelets *p90*; buttonholed eyelets *p91*; stem stitch *p96*; damp stretching *p98*; mitred corners *p101*

hemming

1 Fold in 2 cm (¹³⁄₁₆ in) along each side, and then another 2 cm (¹³⁄₁₆ in) to encase the raw edge.

2 Work mitred corners in each of the corners.

3 Machine sew the hem in place, close to its inside edge.

counted tacking

❶ *Very careful counting is required as this counted tacking sets up the positioning of the drawn thread work.*

1 Fold the fabric in half both ways to find the centre. Using a long piece of pale coloured machine sewing thread, come out at the centre and tack from the centre along one of the folds towards the edge. Go over four threads, under four threads, 65 times (520 threads). This point is the midpoint of the outside edge of one side of the border.

2 Turn and work parallel to the edge. With a new thread and a few backstitches, start at the end of the old thread, and go under and over three threads twice (12 threads).

3 Go under four, over four threads (8 threads). Go under and over three threads, twelve times (72 threads). Go under and over four threads (8 threads). Go under and over three threads, four times (24 threads). Repeat this sequence four more times. Go under and over four threads (8 threads).

4 Turn the corner, heading along the next side of the fabric. Go under four threads, over four (8 threads). Go under three and over three threads, four times (24 threads). Go under four, over four threads (8 threads). Go under three, over three threads, twelve times (72 threads). Repeat this sequence four more times. Go under four, over four threads (8 threads). Go under three and over three threads, twice (12 threads). This is the midpoint of the border on this side of the fabric.

5 Mark the midpoint by taking a stitch towards the edge under four threads. Insert the needle back over the same four threads, so that there is a little stitch jutting out to the side. Continuing on the same line as before, go under three and over three threads, twice (12 threads). Go under four threads, over four threads (8 threads).

6 Go under three threads, over three, twelve times (72 threads). Go under four, over four threads (8 threads). Go under three and over three threads, four times (24 threads). Go under four, over four threads (8 threads). Repeat this sequence four times.

7 Turn the corner, heading along the next side of the fabric. With the same thread, repeat Steps 4-6 to work the tacking along the entire side and mark the midpoint.

8 Work the third side as for the second. For the fourth side, work step 4, finishing at the midpoint of the side. To finish, tack a little to the side and fasten the thread.

9 Remove the initial line of tacking down the fold.

drawn thread work

❶ *For clarity, rows have been assigned a number, and columns a letter on the Pattern Sheet. Intersections are named according to the row and column into which they fall.*

❶ *All drawn thread work is stitched using pearl cotton and the tapestry needle. Use the counted tacking to assist with positioning.*

1 Begin at the magenta arrowhead (1A) and using the counted tacking, count eight threads to the right. Bring the needle out on the tacking line. Work the horizontal bar of nine satin stitches, positioning it according to the chart.

❶ *The inside edge of the bar sits on the tacking guide.*

2 Turn the corner and work the vertical satin stitch bar.

3 Leave the needle and thread ready for later use.

4 With sharp, fine-pointed scissors, cut the eight threads on the inside edge of each of the two satin stitch bars. Work slowly and carefully.

5 With the point of a needle, gently prise up one of the ends of the cut threads next to the first satin stitch bar.

6 Continue in the same way along the thread, levering it up and out, for about 5 cm (2 in).

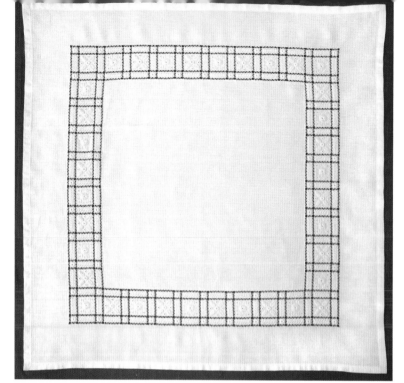

7 Lever each of the other cut threads out, back to the same point.

❶ *Cut them off or pin them out of the way. As you work along the line of stitching, these threads will need to be withdrawn further.*

8 Returning to the working thread, bring it out at the edge of the drawn thread area, six threads along from the end of the satin stitching.

9 Heading from 1A to 2A, work three wiggly bars, stopping one bar from the end. At 2A, work a 'T intersection–opening end ME' to introduce a new thread.

10 Run a new thread under the back of the satin stitch bars at 1A and work three bars from 1A to 1B, stopping one bar from the end.

11 With a new thread, work the satin stitch bar at 1B. Cut and withdraw threads as required. Lace the thread behind the last bar of 1A-1B. Continuing with the previous thread, overcast the final bar of 1A-1B, including the laced thread. Run the thread under the satin stitch bar, and continue on, working eleven bars from 1B to 1C, stopping one bar from the end.

12 Use the same process to introduce a new thread and work the satin stitch bar at 1C, then work along to 1D and repeat the process.

13 Picking up the threads introduced at 1B, 1C and 1D, work three bars towards row 2, stopping one bar before the end of each section.

14 With the new thread introduced at 2A, work bars from 2A to 2B, stopping one bar from the end. Work a 'cross intersection M3'. Work bars from 2B to 2C, stopping one bar from the end. Work a 'cross intersection M3'. Work bars from 2C to 2D, stopping one bar from the end. Work another 'cross intersection M3'.

15 Picking up the threads at 2A, 2B, 2C and 2D, work bars towards row 3. Stop one bar before each section's end.

16 At 3A, work a 'T intersection–opening end ME' to begin a new thread. With the new thread, work bars from 3A to 3B, stopping one bar from the end.

17 At 3B, work a 'cross intersection M3'. Continuing on with the same thread, work bars from 3B to 3C, stopping one bar from the end. Work a another cross intersection. Continuing, work bars from 3C to 3D, stopping one bar from the end. Work another cross intersection.

18 Picking up the threads at 3A, 3B, 3C and 3D, work bars towards row 4. Stop one bar before each section's end.

19 At 4A, work a 'T intersection–opening end ME' to begin a new thread. With the new thread, work bars from 4A to 4B, stopping one bar from the end.

20 At 4B, work a 'cross intersection M3'. Continuing with the same thread, work bars from 4B to 4C, stopping one bar from the end. Work another cross intersection. Work bars from 4C to 4D, stopping one bar from the end. Work another cross intersection.

21 Picking up the threads at 4A, 4B, 4C and 4D, work bars towards row 5. Stop one bar before each section's end.

22 At 5A, work a 'T intersection–opening end ME' to begin a new thread. With the new thread, work bars from 5A to 5B, stopping one bar from the end.

23 At 5B, work a 'cross intersection M3'. With the same thread, work bars from 5B to 5C, stopping one bar from the end. Work a another cross intersection. Work bars from 5C to 5D, stopping one bar from the end.

24 At 5D, work a 'T intersection–closing end W3' to finish off the thread from row 5.

25 With the threads at 5A, 5B, 5C and 5D, work bars towards row 6, stopping one bar before each section's end.

26 At 6A, work a 'T intersection–opening end ME' to begin a new thread. With the new thread, work bars from 6A to 6B, stopping one bar from the end.

27 At 6B, work a 'cross intersection M3'. With the same thread, work bars from 6B to 6C, stopping one bar from the end. Work a another cross intersection. Work bars from 6C to 6D, stopping one bar from the end.

28 At 6D, work a 'T intersection–closing end W3' to finish off the thread from row 6.

29 Continue in the same manner, working methodically up the side of the tablecloth. At row 12, change to working 'T intersection–opening ends M3' to start rows, 'cross intersections W3' for cross intersections and 'T intersection–closing ends WE' to finish rows.

30 At row 19, instead of finishing the row at D, change to working 'cross intersections W3'.

31 At row 22, work the corner with satin stitch bars. Cut and withdraw the threads as required. Work bars from 22A to 22B, stopping one bar from the end. Lace the 21B-22B thread behind the last bar of 22A-22B. Wrap the bar including the laced thread. Trim the laced thread on the back. Work a satin stitch bar at 22B. Cut and withdraw the threads as required.

32 Continue along row 22, finishing off the threads at 22C and 22D in the same way.

33 Turn the work 90 degrees anticlockwise, and continue up the side, working the first half of the side with 'T intersection–opening ends ME', 'cross intersections M3', and 'T intersection–closing ends W3'. For the second half of the side, change to working 'T intersection–opening ends M3', 'cross intersections W3', and 'T intersection–closing ends WE'.

34 Turn the corner to the third side in the same way as to begin the second side. Continue along the third side.

35 Work the fourth side similarly, up to and including the intersections at row F.

36 Work bars from 1F to 1E, 2F to 2E and 3F to 3E. Work bars from 4F to 4E, stopping one from the end. Work the final bar as a direction changing bar. Work the satin stitch bar at 4E. Finish off the thread under the back of the satin stitch. Cut and withdraw threads as required.

37 Picking up the thread from 1F-1E work the satin stitch bar at 1E and finish off the thread under the back of the satin stitch. Cut and withdraw threads as required.

38 Picking up the threads at 1D, 2D and 3D, work bars towards row E, stopping one bar before the end of each section.

39 Picking up the thread at 4D, work twelve bars from 4D to 4E. Turn the corner and work four bars from 4E to 3E. Lace the thread behind the final bar of 3D-3E. Lace the 3F-3E thread behind the first bar of 3E-2E.

40 With the 3D-3E thread, wrap the final bar of 3D-3E including the laced thread. Work twelve bars from 3E to 2E, including the laced thread in the first bar. Trim the laced threads at the back.

41 Lace the thread behind the final bar of 2D-2E. Lace the 2F-2E thread behind the first bar of 2E-1E. With the 2D-2E thread, wrap the final bar of 2D-2E including the laced thread. Continuing with the same thread, work four bars from 2E to 1E, including the laced thread in the first bar. Trim the laced threads at the back.

42 Lace the 2E-1E thread behind the final bar of 1D-1E. With the 1D-1E thread, wrap the final bar of 1D-1E including the laced thread. Finish off the thread by running it under the back of the satin stitch. Trim the laced thread.

43 Remove the tacking.

surface embroidery

❶ *All embroidery is worked with pearl cotton and the No 4 straw needle. If you are not already using a hoop or frame, mount the fabric in one so that it is drum tight.*

1 Using the charts, trace the motifs onto the centre of each drawn thread work fabric square and rectangle. Use the full mini pattern to guide the direction of the bullions in the rectangular panels.

2 Curlicue squares: work the centre buttonhole eyelet, and the bullions radiating out from it. Work the stem stitch curlicues and the corner eyelets.

3 Leafy squares: work the centre eyelet and the curved bullions around it. Work the stem stitch stems and the bullions along each side. Stitch the buttonhole eyelets at the centre of each side.

4 Small squares: Work the centre eyelet and the bullions radiating out from it.

5 Rectangular panels: Work the stem stitch centre line, and the bullions along either side.

6 Damp stretch the embroidery for a crisp finish. ✿

cushion

This sumptuous Oxford cushion has a central panel of embroidery and a border of embroidery on the cushion flange.

difficulty ▪▪▸

size 33 x 33 cm / 13 x 13 in

materials and equipment

- 50 x 50 cm (20 x 20 in) 38 count linen, white
- 3 balls No 8 pearl cotton, white
- No 24 tapestry needle
- No 4 straw needle
- 50 cm (20 in) dupion silk, 112 cm (45 in) wide, red
- 24 x 46 cm (9½ x 18⅛ in) polycotton fabric, white
- 2 buttons, 20 mm (¹³⁄₁₆ in) diameter, to match silk
- machine sewing thread, white and red to match silk
- polyester fibre fill

chart Pattern sheet A

stitches and techniques

counted satin stitch *p48*; cutting threads *p48*; withdrawing threads *p49*; zigzag overcast bars *p74*; turning a corner *p75*; cross filling *p76*; cross intersection M3 *p77*, ME *p78*, W3 *p79*, WE *p80*; T intersection–opening end M3 *p81*, ME *p82*; T intersection–closing end M3 *p83*, ME *p84*; tracing patterns *p86*; bullion knot *p88*; eyelets *p90*; buttonholed eyelets *p91*; stem stitch *p96*; damp stretching *p98*; ladder stitch *p103*

counted tacking

❶ *Very careful counting is required as this counted tacking sets up the positioning of the drawn thread work.*

1 Fold the fabric in half both ways to find the centre.

2 Thread a needle with a long piece of pale coloured machine sewing thread.

3 Tack along the fold toward the bottom fabric edge. Coming up at the centre, go over and under four threads, 29 times (232 threads). Go over four more threads, taking the thread to the back. Leave the ends hanging.

4 Using the counted tacking, count down 31 groups of four threads (124 threads) from the centre. Mark with a pin.

5 Leaving a 30 cm (12 in) tail on a new thread, insert the needle at the pin (corresponding with the inner magenta arrowhead). Remove the pin. Tack parallel with the fabric's bottom edge. Go over and under four threads, 15 times (120 threads). Go over four more threads.

6 Turn the corner and work along the next side, going under four, over four threads, 31 times (248 threads).

7 Work the third and fourth sides in the same way as the second. Tack a little further and fasten the thread.

8 Rethread the long tail from the beginning. Heading in the opposite direction to before, go under and over four threads, 15 times (120 threads). Go under four more threads. Tack a little further and fasten the thread.

9 Leaving a 40 cm (16 in) tail on a new thread, insert the needle at the end of the initial tacking (28 groups of threads from the inner tacked ring, corresponding with the outer magenta arrowhead) and tack parallel with the bottom edge of the fabric. Go over and under four threads, 29 times (232 threads). Go over four more threads.

10 Turn the corner and head along the next side, going under four, over four threads, 59 times (472 threads).

11 Turn the corner and work the third and fourth sides in the same way as the second. Tack a little further and fasten the thread.

12 Rethread the long tail from the beginning. Heading in the opposite direction to before, go under and over four threads, 29 times (232 threads). Go under four more threads. Tack a little further and fasten the thread.

13 Remove the initial line of tacking down the fold.

drawn thread work

❶ *For clarity, rows have been assigned a number, and columns a letter on the Pattern Sheet. Intersections are named according to the row and column into which they fall.*

❶ *All drawn thread work is stitched using pearl cotton and the tapestry needle. Use the counted tacking to assist with positioning.*

❶ *All intersections should be worked with cross fillings. Cross fillings are only mentioned when it is not an intersection with step-by-step instructions elsewhere in the book.*

outer border

1 Begin at the 1A corner and using the counted tacking, count eight threads to the right. Bring the needle out on the tacking line. Work the horizontal bar of nine satin stitches, positioning the bar according to the chart.

❶ *The inside edge of the bar sits on the tacking guide.*

2 Turn the corner and work the vertical satin stitch bar.

3 Leave the needle and thread ready for later use.

4 With sharp, fine-pointed scissors, cut the eight threads on the inside edge of each of the two satin stitch bars. Work slowly and carefully.

5 With the point of a needle, gently prise up one of the ends of the cut threads next to the first satin stitch bar.

6 Continue in the same way along the thread, levering it up and out, for about 5 cm (2 in).

7 Lever each of the cut threads out to the same place.

❶ *Cut them off or pin them out of the way. As you work along the line of stitching, these threads will need to be withdrawn further.*

8 Returning to the working thread, bring it out at the edge of the drawn thread area, four threads up from the end of the satin stitching.

9 Work zigzag bars 1A to 2A. At 2A, work a 'T intersection–opening end M3' to introduce a new thread.

10 With the new thread, work zigzag bars from 2A to 2B.

11 Run a new thread under the back of the vertical satin stitch bar at 1A and work the first half of a cross filling from the bottom left of 1A to the top right. Run the thread under the back of the horizontal satin stitch bar then complete the cross filling. Work zigzag bars from 1A to 1B.

12 With a new thread, work the satin stitch bar at 1B. Cut and withdraw the threads as required. Lace the new thread behind the first bar of 1B-1C. Continuing with the new thread, work the first half of the cross filling from top right to bottom left. Work bars from 1B to 2B.

13 Work a 'cross intersection WE' at 2B.

14 With the 1A-2A and 1B-2B threads, work bars towards row 3, stopping one bar before each section's end.

15 At 3A, work a 'T intersection – opening end ME' to introduce a new thread. With the new thread, work bars from 3A to 3B. At 3B, work a 'T intersection – closing end M3' to finish the thread.

16 With the threads at 3A and 3B, work bars up to row 4.

17 At 4A, work a 'T intersection – opening end M3' to introduce a new thread. With the new thread, work bars from 4A to 4B. At 4B, work a 'T intersection – closing end ME' to finish the thread.

18 With the threads at 4A and 4B, work bars towards row 5, stopping one bar from the end of each section.

19 At 5A, work a 'T intersection – opening end ME' to introduce a new thread. With the new thread, work six bars from 5A to 5B. At 5B, work a 'T intersection – closing end M3' to finish the thread.

20 Picking up the threads at 5A and 5B, work bars up to row 6.

21 At 6A, work a 'T intersection – opening end M3' to introduce a new thread. With the new thread, work bars from 6A to 6B. At 6B, work a 'T intersection – closing end ME' to finish the thread.

22 With the threads at 6A and 6B, work bars towards row 7, stopping one bar from the end of each section.

23 At 7A, work a 'T intersection – opening end ME' to begin a new thread. With the new thread, work bars from 7A to 7B. At 7B, work a 'cross intersection ME'.

24 With the threads at 7A and 7B, work bars up to row 8.

25 At 8A, work the corner with satin stitch bars. Turn the work to begin the new side. Work bars from 8A to 8B. Work the satin stitch bar at 8B. Cut and withdraw threads as required.

26 Using the 7B-8B thread, work the first half of the cross filling from bottom right to top left. Lace the thread behind the first bar of 8B-8C. Using the satin stitch bar thread, work the first bar of 8B-8C, including the laced thread. Work the cross filling's second half with the laced thread, then finish it under the back of the satin stitch.

27 Turn the work 90 degrees anti-clockwise, and work the second side in the same way as the first.

28 Work the third then fourth sides, up to and including working the intersections at 1D and 2D on the fourth side.

29 Work bars from 1D to 1C, and 2D to 2C. Work satin stitch bars at 1C and 2C. Finish the 2D-2C thread under the back of the satin stitch. Cut and withdraw threads as required.

30 Picking up the threads at 1B and 2B, work bars towards column C, stopping one bar from the end.

31 Lace the satin stitch bar thread at 1C under the final bar of 1B-1C. Work the last bar of 1B-1C, including the laced thread. Work the first half of the cross filling at 1C from bottom left to top right (when the chart is the right way up). Finish the 1B-1C thread in the back of the satin stitch.

32 With the laced thread, work the second half of the cross filling from top left to bottom right. Work bars from 1C to 2C. Work the first half of the cross filling from bottom left to top right. Lace the thread behind the final bar of 2B to 2C. Work the final bar of 2B-2C, including the laced thread. Trim the laced thread. Work the second half of the cross filling. Finish the thread by running it under the back of the satin stitch bar.

centre square

1 Begin the corner at 3C in the same way as for the outer border corner at 1A.

2 Work bars from 3C to 4C. At 4C, work a 'T intersection – opening end M3' to introduce a new thread.

3 With the same thread, work bars from 4C to 5C, stopping one bar from the end. At 5C, work a 'T intersection – opening end ME' to begin a new thread.

4 With the same thread as before, work bars from 5C to 6C. At 6C, turn the corner with satin stitch bars. Cut and withdraw the threads as required.

5 Work the remaining bars of 6C to 6D. Work a satin stitch bar at 6D. Cut and withdraw the threads as required.

6 Returning to 3C, run a new thread under the back of the satin stitch bars. Work the bars from 3C to 3D.

7 Work the satin stitch bar at 3D. Cut and withdraw the threads as required. Work the first half of the cross filling from bottom right to top left. Run a new thread under the back of the satin stitch bar and lace the thread behind the first bar of 3D to 3E. With this thread, work the second half of the cross filling.

8 Continuing with the thread, work bars from 3D to 4D.

9 Picking up the thread at 4C, work bars from 4C to 4D. At 4D, work a 'cross intersection WE'.

10 Continuing with the 3D-4D thread, work bars from 4D to 5D, stopping one bar before the end.

11 Picking up the thread at 5C, work bars from 5C to 5D. At 5D, work a 'cross intersection ME'.

12 Continuing with the 4D-5D thread, work bars from 5D to 6D. Work the first half of the cross filling from bottom right to top left. Lace the thread behind the first bar of 6D to 6E.

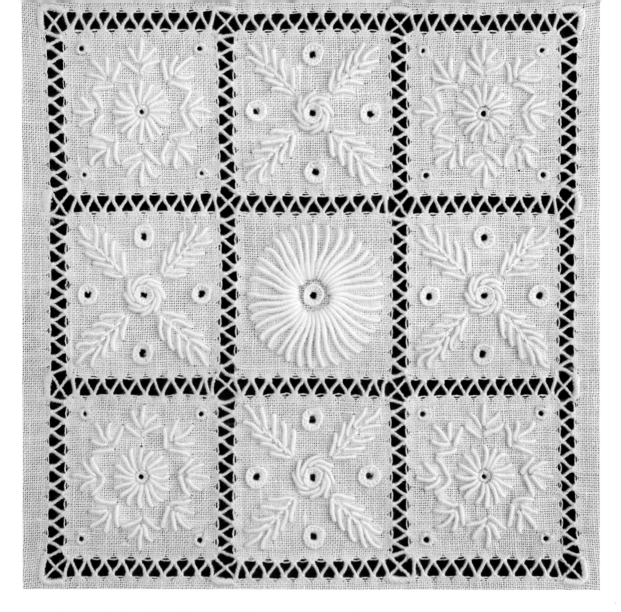

13 Picking up the thread from the satin stitch bar at 6D, work the second half of the cross filling. Work the first bar of 6D to 6E including the laced thread. Trim the laced thread. Work bars from 6D to 6E, stopping one bar before the end.

14 With the thread from 3D, work bars from 3D to 3E, including the laced thread in the first bar, and stopping one bar before the end.

15 With a new thread, work the satin stitch bar at 3E. Cut and withdraw the threads as required. Lace the thread behind the last bar of 3D to 3E. Continuing with the 3D-3E thread, work the last bar, including the laced thread. Run the thread under the back of the satin stitch bar, ready for further stitching later.

16 With the laced thread, work the cross filling's first half from top left to bottom right. Work bars from 3E to 4E.

17 Picking up the thread at 4D, work bars from 4D to 4E, stopping one bar from the end. Work a 'cross intersection W3' at 4E.

18 Continuing with the 3E-4E thread, work bars from 4E to 5E, stopping one bar from the end.

19 Picking up the thread at 5D, work bars from 5D to 5E, stopping one bar from the end. At 5E work a 'cross intersection M3'.

20 With the 4E-5E thread, work bars from 5E to 6E. Lace the thread behind the last bar of 6D-6E, then work a satin stitch bar. Cut and withdraw the threads as required.

21 Continuing with the 6D-6E thread, work the final bar of the section, including the laced thread. Trim the laced thread. Work the first half of the cross filling from top left to bottom right. Run the thread under the back of the satin stitch bar, ready for further stitching later.

22 Work the second half of the cross filling.

23 Picking up the thread at 6E, work bars from 6E to 6F. Work the corner at 6F. Finish the thread under the back of the satin stitch bars.

24 Picking up the thread at 3E, work the first bar of 3E to 3F. Work the second half of the cross filling. Work the remaining bars from 3E to 3F. Work the corner at 3F.

25 Work bars from 3F to 4F. Picking up the thread at 4E, work bars from 4E to 4F. At 4F, work a 'T intersection – closing end ME'.

26 Work bars from 4F to 5F, stopping one bar from the end. With the thread at 5E, work bars from 5E to 5F. At 5F, work a 'T intersection – closing end M3'.

27 Work bars from 5F to 6F. Finish the thread by running it under the back of the satin stitch.

surface embroidery

❶ *All embroidery is worked with pearl cotton and the No 4 straw needle. If you are not already using a hoop or frame, mount the fabric in one so that it is drum tight.*

1 Using the chart, trace the motifs onto the centre of each square and rectangle.

2 Border panels: Stitch the eyelets. Work the radiating bullions starting each one by bringing the needle up adjacent to the eyelet, and inserting the needle at the far end of the stitch. On the rectangles, work the stem stitch, then the curved double bullions down each side.

3 Centre square: work the buttonholed eyelet, then the bullions radiating out from it.

4 Corner squares: Work the eyelets and any radiating bullions. Work the remaining bullion stitches.

5 On the remaining squares, work buttonholed eyelets. Stitch the curved bullions around the centre eyelet. Work the stem stitch, with bullions down each side.

construction

1 Remove the tacking. Damp stretch the embroidery.

2 Count 25 threads out from the border drawn thread area's edge. Using a pale thread, tack around the entire square at this distance away from the drawn thread area.

❶ *The outer stitching line is one thread closer to the centre than the tacking, 24 threads away from the drawn thread area's edge.*

3 Count 25 threads in from the inner edge of the border drawn thread area. Tack around the entire square at this distance away.

❶ *The inner stitching line is one thread further away from the centre than the tacked line, 24 threads away from the drawn thread area's edge.*

4 Measure out 1 cm (⅜ in) from the outer tacking line to create the cutting line. Cut out the embroidery. The panel should measure approximately 36 x 36 cm (14¼ x 14¼ in).

5 Cut a piece of silk fabric, 36 x 36 cm (14¼ x 14¼ in) to match the size of the embroidered cushion front. Lay the embroidery panel face up on top of the silk. Pin the raw edges together and carefully machine stitch, exactly along the outermost tacking line.

6 Cut two pieces of silk 40 x 36 cm (15¾ x 14¼ in). Fold each one in half along the 40 cm (15¾ in) side so that each measures 20 x 36 cm (8 x 14¼ in), with double thickness. Pin or baste the raw edges together.

7 Measure 4 cm (1⅝ in) from the folded edge on one piece, and mark lightly with tailor's chalk at the 4 cm (1⅝ in) mark at several places across the fabric.

8 Lay the other folded piece over it, aligning the fold with the chalk marks. Pin in place and baste the overlap together in the seam allowance (1 cm / ⅜ in seam allowance). This will be the back panel of the cushion.

9 Mark two buttonhole positions on the uppermost back panel, 7 cm (2¾ in) in from the stitching line and 1 cm (⅜ in) away from the folded edge. Work buttonholes to fit your buttons.

10 Position the buttons on the lower back panel, underneath the buttonholes and securely stitch in place.

11 Place the front and the back panels with right sides together. Pin and baste. Using the previous machine stitching on the front panel as a guide, machine stitch just inside it, e.g. 1 mm (¹⁄₃₂ in) or less.

12 Clip the corners to reduce bulk, and turn the cushion cover right side out, through the opening in the back.

13 Press the seams to create a sharp folded edge for the cushion flange.

14 Fasten the buttons in the buttonholes.

15 On the front, using a different pale machine sewing thread, baste the front and back together just inside the inner most tacking from before.

16 One thread out from the first of these two tacking lines, machine stitch using a white top thread, and a bobbin thread that matches the cushion back's fabric.

17 Remove all basting.

inner cushion

1 Fold the polycotton fabric in half, and stitch 1 cm (⅜ in) around the three raw sides, leaving a 5 cm (2 in) gap at one end. Clip the corners and turn the right way out.

2 Fill the cushion with fibre fill. Neatly ladder stitch the gap closed.

3 Unfasten the buttons, insert the inner cushion into the cushion cover, and refasten the buttons. ✥

sampler

This sampler has 36 different bullion stitch motifs, and is an excellent reference for future stitching.

difficulty ▪▪▫

size approximately 31 x 31 cm / 12¼ x 12¼ in

materials and equipment

- 50 x 50 cm (20 x 20 in) 38 count linen, white
- 4 balls No 8 pearl cotton, white
- No 24 tapestry needle
- No 4 straw needle
- Pale coloured machine-sewing thread for tacking

chart Pattern sheet B

stitches and techniques

counted satin stitch *p48*, cutting threads *p48*, withdrawing threads *p49*, straight overcast bars *p51*, turning a corner *p53*, cross intersection *p54*, T intersection – opening end *p55*, T intersection –

closing end *p56*, tracing patterns *p86*, bullion knot *p88*, eyelets *p90*, buttonholed eyelets *p91*, French knots *p92*, padded satin stitch *p94*, stem stitch *p96*, damp stretching *p98*

counted tacking

❶ *Very careful counting is required as this counted tacking sets up the positioning of the drawn thread work.*

1 Measure 9 cm (3⅝ in) along one side from the corner of the fabric. Mark with a pin.

2 From this point, measure 9 cm (3⅝ in) across the fabric. Mark with a pin.

3 Starting at the pin (which corresponds with the arrowhead on the chart), and leaving a 10 cm (4 in) tail of

machine sewing thread for later use, tack parallel with the left edge of the fabric. Go under four threads, over four threads (8 threads). Go under three, over three, twelve times (72 threads). Repeat five more times. Finish the side by going under four threads, over four (8 threads).

4 Turn the corner, heading along the next side of the fabric. Continuing with the same thread, repeat the tacking as for the first side.

5 Work the final two sides in the same way. To finish, tack a little further and fasten the thread.

6 Rethread the long tail from the beginning of the counted tacking. Heading in the opposite direction to before, tack a little further and fasten the thread.

drawn thread work

❶ *For clarity, rows have been assigned a number, and columns a letter on the Pattern Sheet. Intersections are named according to the row and column into which they fall.*

❶ *All drawn thread work is stitched using pearl cotton and the tapestry needle. Use the counted tacking to assist with positioning.*

1 Begin at the magenta arrowhead (1A) and using the counted tacking, count eight threads to the right. Bring the needle out on the tacking line. Work the horizontal bar of nine satin stitches, positioning the bar according to the chart.

❶ *The inside edge of the bar sits on the tacking guide.*

2 Turn the corner and work the vertical satin stitch bar.

3 Leave the needle and thread ready for later use.

4 With sharp, fine-pointed scissors, cut the eight threads on the inside edge of each of the two satin stitch bars. Work slowly and carefully.

5 With the point of a needle, gently prise up one of the ends of the cut threads next to the first satin stitch bar.

6 Continue in the same way along the thread, levering it up and out, for about 5 cm (2 in).

7 Lever each of the other cut threads out, back to the same point.

❶ *Cut them off or pin them out of the way. As you work along the line, the threads will need to be withdrawn further.*

8 Returning to the working thread, bring it out at the edge of the drawn thread area, six threads along from the end of the satin stitching.

9 Work straight bars from 1A to 2A. At 2A, work a 'T intersection – opening end' to introduce a new thread.

10 Continuing on with the same thread, work bars from 2A to 3A. At 3A, work a 'T intersection – opening end' to introduce a new thread.

11 Continue up the A column in the same manner, working twelve straight bars in each section, and introducing a new thread at each T-intersection.

12 At 7A, turn the corner, with satin stitch bars. Cut and withdraw the threads as required.

13 Returning to 1A, run a new thread under the back of the satin stitch bars. Work bars from 1A to 1B.

14 Picking up the threads at 2A, 3A, 4A, 5A, 6A and 7A, work bars in each row across to the B column.

15 At 7B, work a 'T intersection – opening end' to introduce a new thread. With the new thread, work bars from 7B to 6B, stopping one bar from the end.

16 Work a cross intersection at 6B. Keep working bars and cross intersections, down the B column to and including the intersection at 2B.

17 Work bars from 2B to 1B, finishing the row with a 'T intersection – closing end'.

18 Using the thread from 1A to 1B, work bars from 1B to 1C.

19 Picking up the threads at 2B, 3B, 4B, 5B, 6B and 7B, work bars in each row across to the C column.

20 At 7C, work a 'T intersection – opening end' to begin a new thread. With the new thread, work bars from 7C to 6C, stopping one bar from the end.

21 Work a cross intersection at 6C. Keep working bars and cross intersections, down the C column to and including the intersection at 2C.

22 Work bars from 2C to 1C, finishing the row with a 'T intersection – closing end'.

23 With the 1B-1C thread, work bars from 1C to 1D.

24 Picking up the threads at 2C, 3C, 4C, 5C, 6C and 7C, work bars in each row across to the D column.

25 Continue in the same manner, working intersections as you progress down columns, and filling the rows across between the columns, until you reach G7.

26 At G7, turn the corner with satin stitch bars. Cut and withdraw threads as needed. Work eleven bars from G7 to G6, stopping one bar from the end.

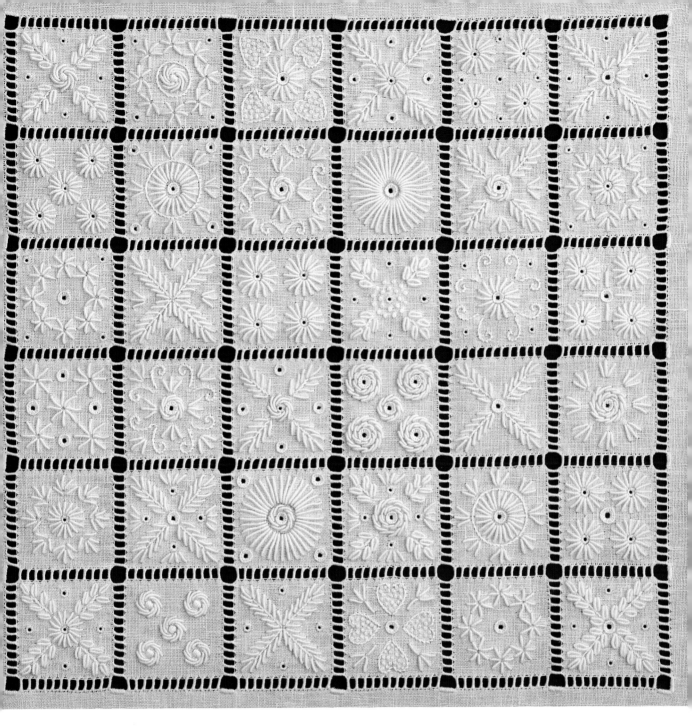

27 Lace the thread F6-G6 thread behind the final bar of G7-G6. Work the final bar, treating the laced thread as one to also be wrapped. Trim the laced thread.

28 Continuing with the thread from G7-G6, work the satin stitch bar at G6. Cut and withdraw the threads as required.

29 Work bars from G6 to G5, stopping one bar from the end.

30 Work the intersection at G5 in the same way as for G6, then continue down G column, overcasting bars and working intersections following the same pattern.

31 At G1, work two satin stitch bars, and finish the thread by running it under the back of the satin stitch.

32 Remove the tacking.

surface embroidery

❶ *All embroidery is worked with pearl cotton and the No 4 straw needle. If you are not already using a hoop or frame, mount the fabric in one so that it is drum tight.*

❶ *Use the photo above as a guide for stitch type and placement.*

1 Using the chart, centre and trace the motifs onto each drawn thread work fabric square.

2 For each square, work any stem stitch first. Next work any padded satin stitch. Work the eyelets and buttonholed eyelets, and any bullions radiating out from them. Stitch any French knots. Work any remaining bullions.

❶ *I usually work an individual square at a time, rather than parts of each across the whole piece.*

3 Damp stretch the embroidery for a crisp finish. ✿

bookmark

The embroidery on this bookmark protrudes from your book's top for all to see and enjoy.

difficulty ♟
size 6.5 x 25.5 cm / 2⅝ x 10 in
materials and equipment

- 35 x 18 cm (14 x 7 in) 38 count linen, white
- 1 ball No 8 pearl cotton, DMC 644 (beige)
- No 24 tapestry needle
- No 4 straw needle
- No 9 embroidery needle
- machine-sewing thread, white

chart Pattern sheet A
stitches and techniques
counted satin stitch p48, cutting threads p48, withdrawing threads p49, wiggly overcast bars p57, turning a corner p59, tracing patterns p86, bullion knot p88, eyelets p90, herringbone stitch p92, ladder stitch p103

embroidery

1 Fold the short side of the fabric in half, and finger press to make a crease.
2 Measure 8 cm (3 in) from the top end, down the crease. Mark with a pin. From the pin, measure 1.2 cm (½ in) out to the right. Mark with a new pin.
3 Thread the tapestry needle with some pearl cotton. Using a waste knot, bring the needle out at the newly pinned point. Remove the pins.
4 The starting point is marked on the chart with a magenta arrowhead. Work the horizontal bar of nine satin stitches, positioning the bar according to the chart.
5 Turn the corner and work the vertical satin stitch bar.
6 With sharp, fine-pointed scissors, slowly and carefully cut the eight threads on the first nine stitches' inside edge.
7 With the point of a needle, gently prise up one of the cut threads, close to the cut end.
8 Continue in the same way along the thread, levering it up and out, for about 2 cm (¾ in).
9 Lever each of the other cut threads out, back to the same point and pin them out of the way.

10 Bring the thread out at the left edge of the drawn thread area, six threads above the end of the satin stitching. Work six wiggly bars.
❶ *Withdraw the threads further as needed, but only to the end of where the wiggly bars will be stitched.*
11 Work two satin stitch bars to turn the corner. Cut the threads inside the corner. Remove the threads from the first side. Draw back the threads for the second side.
12 Following the chart, complete the drawn thread work.
13 Trace the motif onto the centre of the square.
❶ *If you are not already using a hoop or frame, mount the fabric in one so that it is drum tight.*
14 Change to the straw needle. Work the eyelet. Work the bullion stitches radiating out from the central eyelet, starting each one by bringing the needle up adjacent to the eyelet, and inserting the needle at the far end of the stitch.

finishing

1 Measure out 3 cm (1¼ in) from the edge of the drawn thread areas at the top and side edges. Mark with pins.
2 Measure 22 cm (8½ in) from the bottom edge of the drawn thread area, down the length of the bookmark, and mark with a pin.
❶ *The pinned points mark the cutting lines.*
3 Trim the fabric at these points. Carefully cut along a single fabric thread on each side so that it is cut straight.
4 Fold 6 mm (¼ in) to the front along the top and bottom edges. Press gently with an iron. Fold in another 6 mm (¼ in) to encase the raw edge and create the hem. Press again.
5 Baste in place with the machine sewing thread.
6 Starting at the centre of the sides, fold in 6 mm (¼ in), and then another 6 mm (¼ in) to create the hem. Press.
❶ *To slightly reduce bulk in the corners, open out the side folds. Trim the corner of the fabric as shown, then refold the top down, and the side in.*
7 Baste the hem corners in place.
8 Using white machine sewing thread, ladder stitch along the doubled edges of the corner folds.
9 With pearl cotton, work herringbone stitch over the edge of the hem fold to create a decorative hem.
❶ *The height of the stitch shown is about 5 mm (³⁄₁₆ in).*
10 Remove the basting. ✢

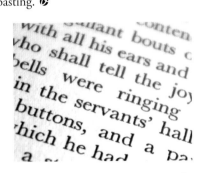

hand towel

A hand towel like this is almost too pretty to use, but linen makes a lovely thirsty towel.

difficulty ▨▨

size 40 x 60 cm / 16 x 24 in

materials and equipment

- 45 x 65 cm (18 x 26 in) 38 count linen, white, cut straight with the grain of the fabric
- 1 ball No 8 pearl cotton, white
- No 24 tapestry needle
- No 4 straw needle
- white and pale coloured machine-sewing thread

chart Pattern sheet B

stitches and techniques

counted satin stitch *p48*; cutting threads *p48*: withdrawing threads *p49*: wiggly overcast bars *p57*: turning a corner *p59*: T intersection – opening end M3 *p64*, ME *p65*; T intersection – closing end M3 *p66*, ME *p67*; tracing patterns *p86*; bullion knot *p88*; eyelets *p90*; herringbone stitch *p92*; padded satin stitch *p94*; sham hem stitch *p95*; stem stitch *p96*; wide stem stitch *p96*; damp stretching *p98*; ladder stitch *p103*

counted tacking

❶ *Very careful counting is required as this counted tacking sets up the positioning of the drawn thread work.*

1 Fold one of the short sides of the fabric in half to find the centre. Finger press along the fold.

2 Measure 12 cm (5 in) from the edge along the fold. Mark with a pin.

3 Starting at the pin (corresponding with the magenta arrowhead on the chart), and leaving a long tail of machine sewing thread, tack parallel with the short side of the fabric. Go under three threads, over three, six times (36 threads). Go under and over four (8 threads). Go under and over three, four times (24 threads). Go under four threads, over four (8 threads). Go under three, over three, 12 times (72 threads). Go under four, over four (8 threads). Go under three, over three, four times (24 threads). Go under four threads, over four (8 threads).

4 Turn the corner, heading further into the main body of the fabric. With the same thread, go under four threads, over four (8 threads). Go under three, over three, 12 times (72 threads). Go under four, over four (8 threads).

5 Turn the corner, heading back across the fabric, parallel to the first tacking line. Continuing with the same thread, go under four threads, over four (8 threads). Go under three, over three, four times (24 threads). Go under four, over four (8 threads). Go under three, over three, 12 times (72 threads). Go under four, over four (8

threads). Go under three, over three, four times (24 threads). Go under four, over four (8 threads). Go under three, over three, 12 times (72 threads). Go under four, over four (8 threads). Go under three, over three, four times (24 threads). Go under four threads, over four (8 threads). Go under three, over three, 12 times (72 threads). Go under four, over four (8 threads). Go under three, over three, four times (24 threads). Go under four threads, over four (8 threads).

6 Turn the corner. With the same thread, go under four threads, over four (8 threads). Go under three, over three, 12 times (72 threads). Go under four, over four (8 threads). Tack a little further and fasten the thread.

7 Rethread the long tail from the beginning of the counted tacking. Heading in the opposite direction to before, go over three threads, under three threads, six times (36 threads). Go over four, under four threads (8 threads). Go over three, under three, four times (24 threads). Go over four, under four (8 threads). Go over three, under three, 12 times (72 threads). Go over four, under four (8 threads). Go over three, under three, four times (24 threads). Go over four, under four (8 threads). Tack a little further and fasten the thread.

drawn thread work

❶ *For clarity, rows have been assigned a number, and columns a letter on the Pattern Sheet. Intersections are named according to the row and column into which they fall.*

❶ *All drawn thread work is stitched using pearl cotton and the tapestry needle. Use the counted tacking to assist with positioning.*

1 From 1A corner, use the counted tacking to count eight threads to the right. Bring the needle out on the tacking line. Work the horizontal bar of nine satin stitches, positioning it according to the chart.

❶ *The inside edge of the bar sits on the tacking guide.*

2 Turn the corner and work the vertical satin stitch bar.

3 With sharp, fine-pointed scissors, cut the eight threads on the inside edge of each of the two satin stitch bars. Work slowly and carefully.

4 With the point of a needle, gently prise up one of the ends of the cut threads next to the first satin stitch bar.

5 Continue in the same way along the thread, levering it up and out, for about 5 cm (2 in).

6 Lever each of the cut threads out to the same place.

❶ *Cut them off or pin them out of the way. As you work along the line, the threads will need to be withdrawn further.*

7 Returning to the working thread, bring it out at the edge of the drawn thread area, six threads along from the end of the satin stitching.

8 Work wiggly bars from 1A to 2A. At 2A, turn the corner with satin stitch bars. Cut and withdraw the threads as required.

9 Work bars from 2A to 2B. At 2B, work a 'T intersection – opening end M3' to begin a new thread. With the new thread, work bars from 2B to 1B.

10 At 1A, run a new thread under the back of the satin stitch bars. Work bars from 1A to 1B. At 1B, work a 'T intersection – closing end ME'.

11 Picking up the threads at 1B and 2B, work bars to 1C and 2C respectively, stopping one bar before the end.

12 At 2C, work a 'T intersection – opening end ME' to begin a new thread. Work bars from 2C to 1C. At 1C, work a 'T intersection – closing end M3'.

13 Picking up the threads at 1C and 2C, work bars to 1D and 2D respectively.

14 At 2D, work a 'T intersection – opening end M3' to begin a new thread. Work bars from 2D to 1D. At 1D, work a 'T intersection – closing end ME'.

15 Continue working bars along rows 1 and 2, alternating between M3 and ME opening and closing intersections for each column. Work bars right up to column H.

16 At 2H, work a corner. Work bars from 2H to 1H. Work a corner. Finish off both threads by running them under the back of the satin stitch bars.

surface embroidery

❶ *All embroidery is worked with pearl cotton and the No 4 straw needle. If you are not already using a hoop or frame, mount the fabric in one so that it is drum tight.*

1 Trace the motifs onto the squares and rectangular panels.

2 Work the wide stem stitch in the centre of each rectangular panel. Follow the chart, and work it as a counted stitch. Work the bullions down each side.

3 On the centre square, work the eyelets. Work the radiating bullion stitches, starting each one by bringing the needle up adjacent to the eyelet, and inserting the needle at the far end of the stitch.

4 On the side squares, work the padded satin stitch centre. Work the stem stitch circles, then the swirling bullions. Work the remaining bullions and the corner eyelets.

5 Work the first layer stitches for the sham hem stitch, along the top and the bottom of the embroidered panel. Follow the chart on the pattern sheet for stitch placement. Work the second layer on the return journey.

finishing

1 Fold 12 mm (½ in) to the front, along the top and bottom edges. Press with an iron. Fold in another 12 mm (½ in) to encase the raw edge and create the hem. Press again.

2 Baste in place with the machine sewing thread.

3 Starting at the centre of the sides, fold in 12 mm (½ in), and then another 12 mm (½ in) to create the hem. Press.

❶ *To slightly reduce bulk in the corners, open out the side folds. Trim the corner of the fabric as shown, then refold the top down, and the side in.*

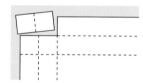

4 Baste the hem corners in place.

5 Using white machine sewing thread, neatly ladder stitch the doubled edges of the corner folds together.

6 With pearl cotton, work herringbone stitch over the edge of the hem fold to create a decorative hem.

❶ *The height of the stitch shown is about 5 mm (⅜ in).*

7 Remove the basting. Damp stretch the embroidery. ✿

drawn thread work

Portuguese whitework is worked in two distinct stages. First, a framework of drawn thread work is completed, and then onto the framework, the surface embroidery is stitched. The drawn thread work is worked first so as to ensure accurate later placement of the surface embroidery.

The drawn thread work consists of overcast (or wrapped) bars, of which there are three types: straight, wiggly and zigzag. Each method creates a different visual effect.

counted satin stitch

The ends of the drawn thread areas are worked in satin stitch to provide a neat edge to the cut threads. Use a tapestry needle so that it goes between the threads instead of splitting them.

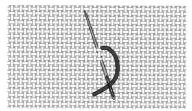

1 Bring the thread out of the fabric. Insert it three threads below. Bring it out again one thread to the left of where it first emerged.

2 Pull the needle through. Insert it three threads below again. Bring it out one thread to the left of where it last emerged.

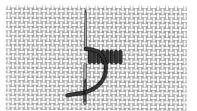

3 Work until there are eight parallel satin stitches. Work the ninth stitch, and bring the needle out again in the same hole as where it last emerged.

❶ *If you are working a single bar of satin stitch, take the needle to the back and finish the thread off by running it through the back of the satin stitch.*

4 Pull the needle through. Turn the work 90 degrees anticlockwise. Insert the needle three threads below. Bring it out again one thread to the left of where it last emerged.

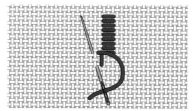

5 Pull the needle through. Insert it three threads below again. Bring it out one thread to the left of where it last emerged.

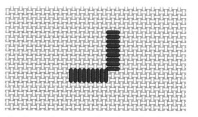

6 Complete another band of nine satin stitches.

❶ *Either leave the thread hanging on the back ready to start the overcast bars, or finish it off by running it through the back of the satin stitch.*

cutting threads

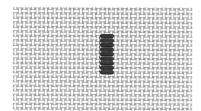

1 Adjacent to the nine satin stitches, there are eight fabric threads that need to be cut: the eight threads between the stitches.

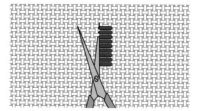

2 With the satin stitch on the right, carefully slip the blade of the scissors in under the top two threads to be cut. Bring the scissor tip back to the front of the fabric.

❶ *This will ensure that you do not cut more threads than you intend.*

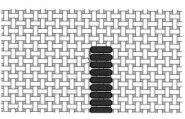

3 Give the scissors a little wiggle to check that none of the stitching thread is caught on the blades. Carefully snip the fabric threads as close as possible to the stitches, without disturbing the stitches.

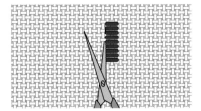

4 Move down to the next two threads and carefully cut them in the same way.

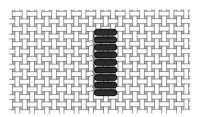

5 Continue until all eight threads are cut.

❶ *If you prefer, you can cut in groups of four threads, rather than groups of two. Don't try doing all eight at once though!*

withdrawing threads

Once the threads are cut they need to be withdrawn to create the drawn thread area.

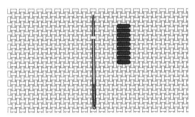

1 Insert the tapestry needle under one of the cut threads, a short distance away from where it was snipped.

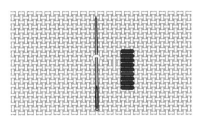

2 Gently lever the thread end up and out of the fabric.

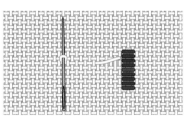

3 Move further along the same thread and repeat, withdrawing as much of the thread as is needed.

❶ *The far end of the thread will also have a satin stitch bar, at which point the thread will be cut too. Usually you won't want or need to withdraw the threads right back to that point until later. The longer the threads stay in place in the fabric, the more stable the fabric will be.*

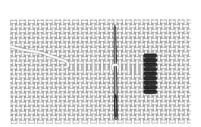

4 Adjacent threads should also be withdrawn.

❶ *After thread removal sometimes thread fuzz or fluff remains amongst the fabric threads. Pick it out with your fingers or tweezers so it doesn't make the wrapped bars look fuzzy and ill-defined.*

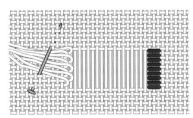

5 Pin the withdrawn threads out of the way.

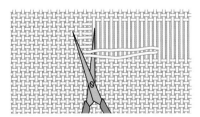

❶ *If you're out in the middle of a long drawn thread area, the withdrawn threads can be cut off. However, if you're close to the end of a line, it is better to simply pin them out of the way.*

starting and finishing threads

The easiest place to finish an old thread and start a new one is in adjacent satin stitch. However, sometimes this is not possible if you run out of thread some distance away.

The technique is shown with wiggly overcast bars, but is worked similarly for the other types of overcast bars.

The old thread is shown in red, and the new in blue.

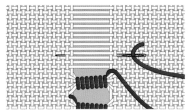

1 When there is enough thread to do only one more bar, knot the end of a new thread and thread it into another needle. Insert it from the front of the fabric, level with the middle of the next bar, two threads away from the drawn thread area. Bring it out in the corresponding position on the other side and leave it hanging.

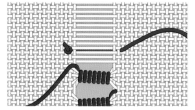

❶ *The knotted end should be at the side where the old thread is. The new thread hangs from the end of the bar where the old thread will finish once it has wrapped its last bar.*

Above shows what it would be like if the zigzag were going the other direction.

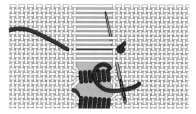

2 With the old thread, begin the next bar as you would normally, making sure that the needle catches in the new thread along with the six fabric threads.

❶ *The new thread laced across the back will be treated as an extra thread in the bar, and wrapped along with them.*

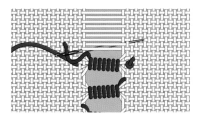

3 Wrap the remainder of the bar as usual, including the laced thread. Finish the thread by catching it at the side and bringing it out at the far end of the next bar in the fabric.

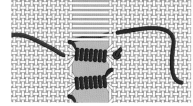

4 Pull the needle through and unthread it.

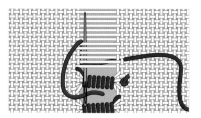

5 Pull the new thread back through to the underside, from where it was left hanging at the end of the previous bar. Rethread it and bring it out ready to work the new bar.

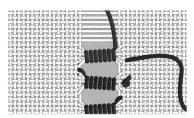

6 With the new thread, wrap the bar, including the old thread laced across the back with the rest of the six threads.

7 At the completion of the bar, the knot from the new thread and the tail of the old thread can be carefully cut off, and stitching can continue as normal.

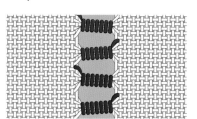

8 The seamless transition from old thread to new.

straight overcast bars

These bars are usually worked over groups of six threads, across a width of eight withdrawn threads. Because all bars are worked in the same direction, they all lie neatly parallel.

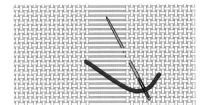

1 Remove eight threads from the fabric to create the drawn thread area. Bring the needle out one thread to the left of it. Insert the needle level with this, one thread to the right of the drawn thread area. Bring the needle out again in the drawn thread area, three threads above.

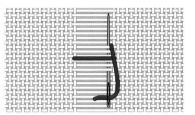

2 Pull the needle through. From below and a little to the left, slide the needle under those same three threads and the three below it (six threads in total).

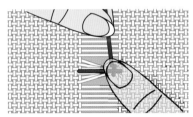

3 To tighten the stitch, pinch the stitch between your forefinger and thumb, and pull the thread away from it with the other hand.

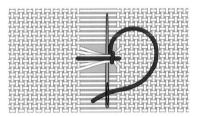

4 A little to the left, slide the needle under the same six threads, from below.

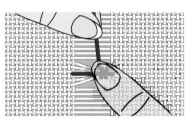

5 Make sure the new stitch sits next to the previous one, rather than on top of it, and then pinch and pull to tighten.

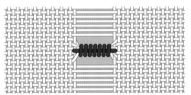

6 Continue similarly, wrapping and tightening to fill the bar, ending with the thread at the back of the fabric.
❶ *Ensure the tension is consistent across the bar.*

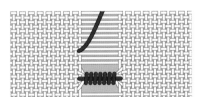

7 Working with the next group of six threads, bring the needle out one thread left of the drawn thread area, halfway up the group of six.

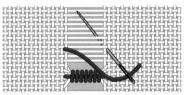

8 Insert the needle level with this, one thread to the right of the drawn thread area. Bring the needle out again in the drawn thread area, three threads above.

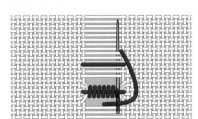

9 Pull the needle through. From below and a little to the left, slide the needle under the six threads of the group.

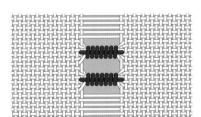

10 Complete the rest of the bar, ending with the thread at the back.
❶ *For consistency, all bars should have the same quantity of wraps.*

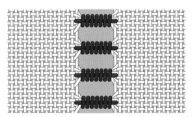

11 Continue in the same way to work the rest of the drawn thread area as required.
❶ *These bars can also be worked in mirror image, lacing from right to left, then filling the bar left to right.*

straight bars: changing direction

It is sometimes necessary to change direction when working complicated drawn thread areas. A change of direction mid-section can be noticeable, so only change direction at the beginning or end of a section of drawn thread work.

at the beginning of a section

Sometimes you will come to a section on a particular side, but you may not want to work that section starting on that side. In that case you will need to change directions at the beginning of the section.

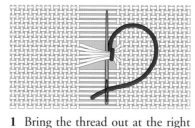

1 Bring the thread out at the right edge of the drawn thread area, and wrap the bar travelling from right to left.

❶ *If your bar is to be wrapped left to right (which it may be), you will need to work the opposite of what is shown here.*

2 To finish, slide the needle under the bar and bring the needle out one thread left of the drawn thread area, halfway up the next group of six.

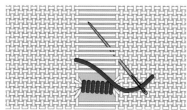

3 Pull the needle through. Lace from left to right, inserting the needle level with where it emerged, one thread to the right of the drawn thread area. Bring the needle out again in the drawn thread area, three threads above.

4 Wrap the bar, travelling from right to left. To finish, slide the needle under the bar and bring the needle out one thread left of the drawn thread area, halfway up the next group of six. Continue lacing and wrapping bars as required.

at the end of a section

You can change direction at the end of a section if you would otherwise end up in a dead end.

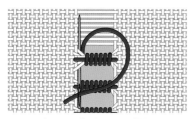

1 Work straight bars to fill the area required, until the second last bar. Finish it with the needle at the front.
❶ *If the last bar is to be worked right to left (which it may be), you will need to work the opposite of what is shown here.*

2 Pull the needle through. Catch the thread between the two bars by inserting the needle one thread to the left, level with the gap above the bar, then bring the needle out up six threads, in the drawn thread area.

3 Wrap the bar, travelling from left to right. When finished, take the thread to the back.

straight bars: turning a corner

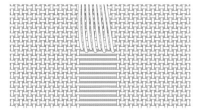

1 Withdraw the threads to where the overcast bars will end.

❶ *This will mean that the fabric remains intact for sewing the satin stitch bars. Otherwise it would be less stable and harder to stitch.*

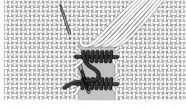

2 Work up to the corner. Bring the needle out one thread left and five threads above the end of the laced thread of the final bar.

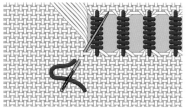

3 Pull the needle and thread through. Turn the work 90 degrees anticlockwise. Insert the needle one thread to the right, bringing it out again in the drawn thread area to the left of the final overcast bar.

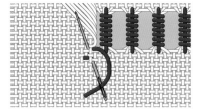

4 Pull the needle and thread through. Insert the needle three threads below. Bring it out three above and one left.

❶ *The short "extra" stitch will be covered by satin stitch. It makes the first satin stitch sit properly, rather than just slipping around the corner from behind the overcast bar.*

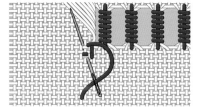

5 Pull the needle and thread through. Moving one thread left, work another satin stitch.

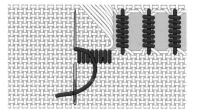

6 Work until there are eight parallel satin stitches. Work the ninth stitch, and bring the needle out again in the hole through which it just emerged.

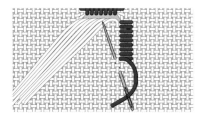

7 Pull the needle and thread through. Turn the work 90 degrees anticlockwise. Insert the needle three threads below, bringing it out one thread left of where it last emerged.

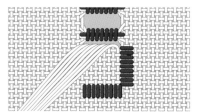

8 Complete another bar of nine satin stitches, and leave the thread hanging on the back, ready to work with it again.

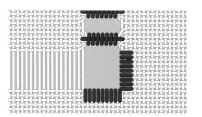

9 Cut the threads inside the corner, adjacent to the satin stitch bars. Remove the already partially withdrawn threads. Draw back the horizontal ones in preparation for bars.

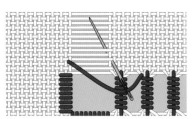

10 Turn the work 90 degrees clockwise. Continue working straight bars as before.

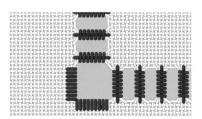

11 The completed corner.

straight bars: cross intersection

The two lines of overcast bars are shown in different colours for clarity.

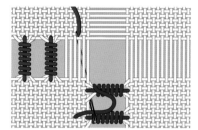

1 Work both lines of overcasting. Stop the blue line one bar before the intersection. Work the red line right up to the intersection. To finish the red bar, take the needle under the bar, bringing it out one thread beyond the unworked blue bar.

2 Pull the red needle and thread through and leave it hanging for further use later on.

3 Picking up the blue thread, work the final blue bar, including the laced red thread. To finish, bring it out one thread beyond the end of the middle of the next unwrapped red bar.

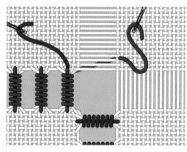

4 Pull the needle and blue thread through and leave it hanging for later use.

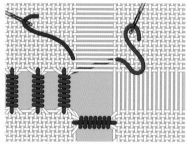

5 Pull the red thread through to the back. Bring it out one thread left of the centre of the next unwrapped red bar.

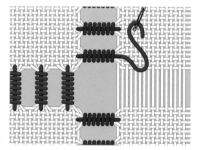

6 Continue overcasting red bars in the same way as before.

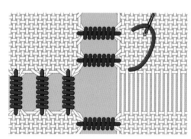

7 Pull the blue thread back through to the back. Bring it out one thread above the centre of the next blue bar.

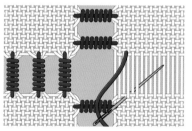

8 Continue overcasting the blue bars in the same way as before.

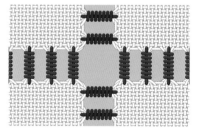

9 The completed cross intersection.

straight bars: t intersection – opening end

The two lines of overcast bars are shown in different colours for clarity.

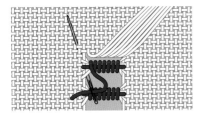

1 Work up to the place where the intersection will begin, having withdrawn the threads only to the end of the overcast bars. Bring the needle out one thread left and five threads above the end of the laced thread of the final bar.

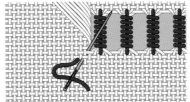

2 Pull the needle and thread through. Turn the work 90 degrees anticlockwise. Insert the needle one thread to the right, bringing it out again in the drawn thread area to the left of the final overcast bar.

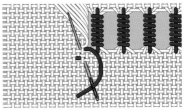

3 Pull the needle and thread through. Insert the needle three threads below. Bring it out three above and one left.

❶ *The short 'extra' stitch will be covered by satin stitch. It makes the first satin stitch sit properly, rather than just slipping around the corner from behind the overcast bar.*

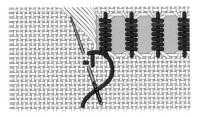

4 Pull the needle and thread through. Moving one thread left, work another satin stitch.

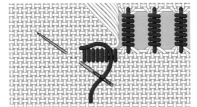

5 Work eight satin stitches. Insert the needle for the ninth stitch. Bring it out three threads left and two up, ready to begin the next overcast bar.

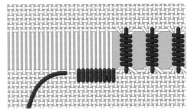

6 Pull the needle and thread through and leave them hanging for further use later. Withdraw the fabric threads further towards the left.

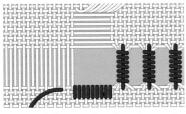

7 Carefully cut the threads on the inside edge of the satin stitch bar, and draw them back a little way.

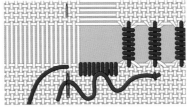

8 Thread a needle with a new knotted thread. From the front, insert it one thread below the red thread. Bring it out directly above, two threads beyond the drawn thread area.

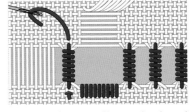

9 Pull the needle and thread through. Treating the laced blue thread as another thread to be overcast, work another red overcast bar.

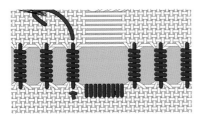

10 Continue on with the red overcast bars.

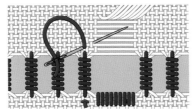

11 Take the blue thread to the back through the hole it came out of, and bring the needle out one thread up and two right.

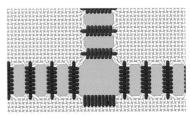

12 Work blue overcast bars in the new drawn thread area. Cut off the knot at the beginning of the thread.

straight bars: t intersection – closing end

The two lines of overcast bars are shown in different colours for clarity. The blue line will be ending, and the red line will be continuing.

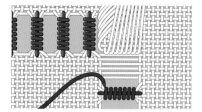

1 Withdraw the threads up to the intersection. Work the blue bars up to this point, leaving the thread hanging on the back for further use later. Work the red line up to one bar away from the intersection.

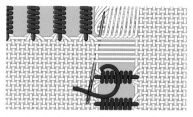

2 Catch the thread between the two bars by inserting the needle three threads above the end of the laced thread of the previous bar, then bring the needle out above the next six threads, in the drawn thread area.

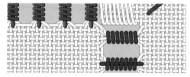

3 Wrap the bar from left to right, bringing the thread out again two threads right and up from the end of the drawn thread area.
❶ *Move the withdrawn threads out of the way if necessary.*

4 Insert the needle one thread below, bringing it out again in the drawn thread area beside the final overcast bar.

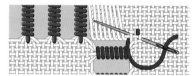

5 Pull the needle and thread through. Insert the needle three threads to the right, and bring it out again one above where it previously emerged.
❶ *The 'extra' stitch will be covered. It makes the first satin stitch sit properly, rather than just slipping around the corner from behind the overcast bar.*

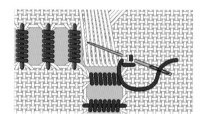

6 Pull the needle and thread through. Moving one thread up, work another satin stitch.

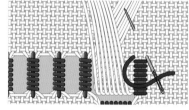

7 Work eight satin stitches. Insert the needle for the ninth stitch. Bring it out three threads left and six up, ready to begin the next overcast bar.

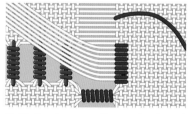

8 Pull the needle and thread through and leave them hanging for further use later. Withdraw the vertical fabric threads further upwards.

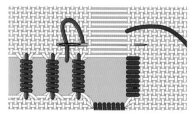

9 Cut the threads from the inside edge of the satin stitch. Remove them. Bring the needle out one thread right and two up from the blue laced thread's end. Insert it one thread right and bring it out at the far side of the next bar.

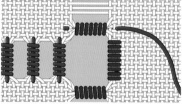

10 Pull the needle through and leave the thread hanging. Continuing with the red thread, wrap the bar from right to left.

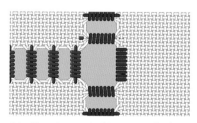

11 Continue stitching straight bars as before. Trim the end of the blue thread.

wiggly overcast bars

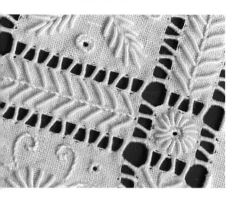

These bars are worked across the drawn thread area and then back for the next one. Even with the most careful stitching they tend to end up slightly angled. Again, they are worked over groups of six threads.

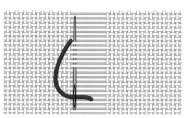

1 Remove eight fabric threads to create the drawn thread area. Bring the needle out at the left side of the drawn thread area, at the top of the first group of six threads. From below, slide the needle under the six threads.

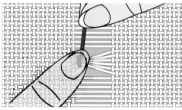

2 Pull the needle through. To tighten the stitch, pinch the stitch between your forefinger and thumb, and pull the thread away from it with the other hand.

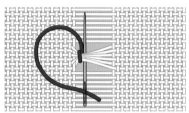

3 A little to the right, slide the needle under the same six threads, from below.

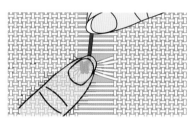

4 Make sure the new stitch sits next to the previous one, rather than on top of it, and then pinch and pull to tighten.

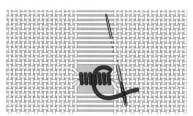

5 Continue similarly, wrapping and tightening with consistent tension, to fill the bar. Insert the needle one thread to the right, level with the gap above the bar. Bring the needle out six threads above, in the drawn thread area.

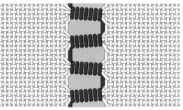

❶ *The stitch to catch the thread at the side makes a neat journey between the two bars. Without out it, the thread would show (as demonstrated above), and therefore not look so neat.*

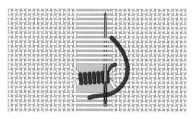

6 Pull the needle through. From below, slide it under the six threads above the previous bar.

7 To tighten the stitch, pinch the stitch between your forefinger and thumb, and pull the thread away from it with the other hand.

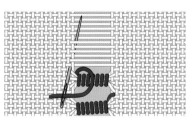

8 Wrap the rest of the bar with the same stitch quantity as the previous bar, making sure the tension is consistent. Insert the needle one thread to the left, level with the gap above the bar. Bring the needle out six threads above, in the drawn thread area.

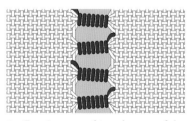

9 Continue, working the rest of the drawn thread area as required.
❶ *For consistency, all bars should have the same quantity of wraps.*

wiggly bars: changing direction

Sometimes it is necessary to change direction when working complicated drawn thread areas. Because these bars zigzag back and forth, a change in the middle is noticeable. For that reason only change direction at the beginning or the end of a section of drawn thread work.

at the beginning of a section

At times the working thread comes to a new section on the opposite side to which you would like to work that section. In that case you will need to change directions at the beginning of the section.

1 Lace from left to right, inserting the needle level with where it emerged, one thread to the right of the drawn thread area. Bring the needle out again in the drawn thread area, three threads above.

❶ *If your bar is to be wrapped right to left (which it may be), you will need to work the opposite of what is shown here.*

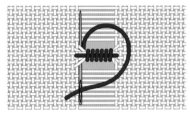

2 Wrap the bar from right to left, with the needle finishing at the front of the fabric.

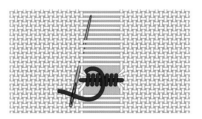

3 Catch the thread between the two bars, then bring the needle out above the next six threads.
❶ *This will mean that two consecutive bars will start from the same end, thereby changing direction.*

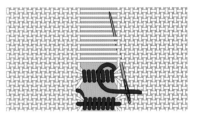

4 Wrap the bar from left to right. Insert the needle one thread to the right, level with the gap above the bar. Bring the needle out six threads above, in the drawn thread area. Continue working bars back and forth.

at the end of a section

You can change direction at the end of a section if you would otherwise end up in a dead end.

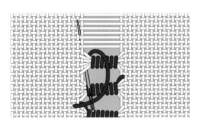

1 Work a regular wiggly bar by wrapping from right to left. To finish, slide the needle under the bar and bring the needle out one thread left of the drawn thread area, halfway up the next group of six.
❶ *If your bar is worked left to right (which it may be), you will need to work the opposite of what is shown here.*

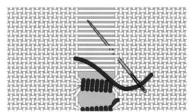

2 Pull the needle through. Lace from left to right, inserting the needle level with where it emerged, one thread to the right of the drawn thread area. Bring the needle out again in the drawn thread area, three threads above.

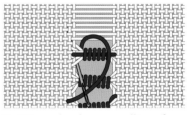

3 Wrap the bar, travelling from right to left. When finished, take the thread to the back.

wiggly bars: turning a corner

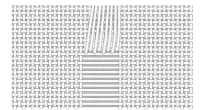

1 Withdraw the threads to where the overcast bars will end.

❶ *This will mean that the fabric remains intact for sewing the satin stitch bars. If the threads were withdrawn further, it would be less stable and harder to stitch.*

2 Stitch up to the corner. To finish the final bar, slide the needle under the bar, bringing the needle out two threads left and up from the top of the last group of six threads.

❶ *The last bar will need to finish on the left, so you may need to work a direction-changing bar to enable this.*

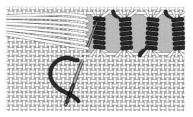

3 Turn the work 90 degrees anti-clockwise. Pull the needle and thread through. Insert the needle one thread to the right. Bring it out in the drawn thread area to the left of the last overcast bar.

❶ *This little stitch will be covered over by the satin stitch bar. It makes the transition between the overcast bar and the satin stitch bar neater.*

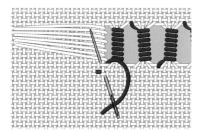

4 Insert the needle three threads below, bringing it out again one thread left of where the thread last emerged.

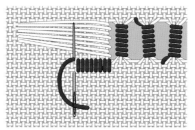

5 Complete a satin stitch bar of nine stitches. To finish the bar and start the next, bring the needle out in the same hole again.

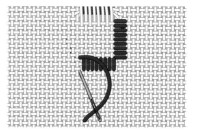

6 Turn the work 90 degrees anti-clockwise, and move the withdrawn thread ends out of the way. Stitch a bar of nine satin stitches for the other side of the corner. Finish with the thread at the back of the fabric.

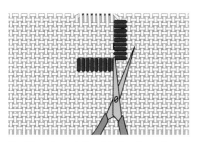

7 Cut the eight fabric threads on the inside edge of each satin stitch bar.

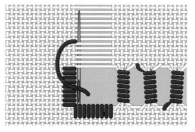

8 Turn the work 90 degrees clockwise. Remove the hanging withdrawn threads, and draw back the newly cut ones to allow for the new line of overcast bars. Bring the needle out six threads up in the drawn thread area, and begin the new bar.

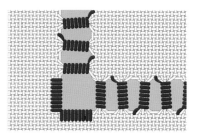

9 Continue stitching overcast bars in the same way as before.

wiggly bars: cross intersections

The two lines of overcast bars are shown in different colours for clarity. There are four different variations of these intersections because of the way the wiggles meet.

M3 variation

The blue line makes an M beside the intersection. The red line makes a 3 above and below the intersection.

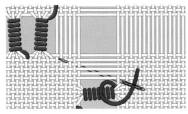

1 Work both lines of overcasting to one bar before the intersection. The blue line finishes at the top, and the red line finishes on the right. Leave the threads hanging for later use. With the red thread coming out above the wrapped bar, insert the needle one thread to the right. Bring it out three threads further on from the end of the unwrapped bar, and two down from the drawn thread area.

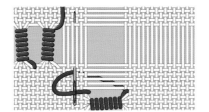

2 Pull the needle and thread through. Insert the needle one thread above. Bring it out again one thread further on from the unwrapped blue bar.

❶ *The laced red thread should have gentle tension, so that when it is bound into the bars, it does not pull too tight.*

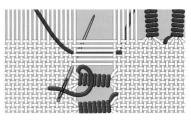

3 Pull the needle and red thread through. Turn the work 90 degrees anticlockwise. With the blue thread coming out above the wrapped bar, insert the needle one thread to the left. Bring it out in the open intersection.

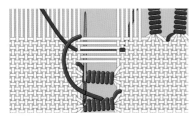

4 Pull the needle and thread through. Wrap the blue bar from left to right, treating the laced red thread as an extra thread to be overcast.

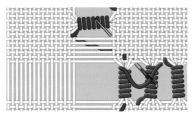

5 Turn the work 90 degrees anticlockwise. To finish the blue bar, slide the needle from the space between the two last blue bars to the space below the last wrapped red bar.

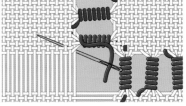

6 Wrap the last bar in the red line from right to left. Finish the bar and bring the needle out three threads further on from the end of the bar, and two threads above the adjacent drawn thread area.

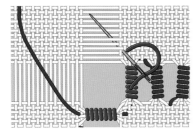

7 Turn the work 90 degrees clockwise. Pull the needle and thread through. Insert the needle one thread left, bringing it out in the drawn thread area, three threads up. Continue overcasting as before.

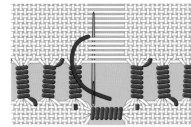

8 Turn the work 90 degrees clockwise. Pull the red thread back through to the back. Bring it out in the drawn thread area, six threads away from the open square, and continue overcasting bars in the red line.

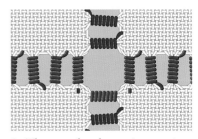

9 The completed cross intersection.

ME variation

The blue line makes an M beside the intersection. The red line makes an E above and below the intersection.

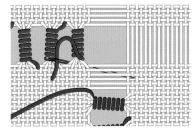

1 Work both lines of overcasting. Finish the red line on the left, one bar before the intersection. Work the blue line right up to the intersection, ending at the bottom. Bring the blue thread out halfway down and one thread right of the unworked red bar.

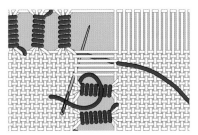

2 Pull the needle and thread through, and leave hanging for later use. Picking up the red thread, insert the needle one thread left of the gap between the bars. Bring the needle out in the intersection opening, treating the laced blue thread as an extra thread to be overcast.

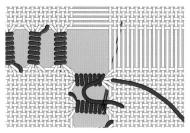

3 Wrap the bar from left to right. Finish the bar by sliding the needle under the bar and bringing it out one thread on from the far end of the adjacent bar, three threads across.

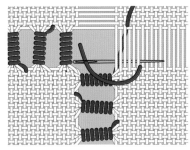

4 Pull the needle and red thread through and leave it hanging for further use later on. Pull the blue thread back through to the back. Bring it out in the drawn thread area, six threads away from the intersection, and continue overcasting bars in the blue line.

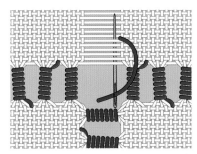

5 Pull the red thread back through to the back. Bring it out in the drawn thread area, six threads away from the intersection, and continue overcasting bars in the red line.

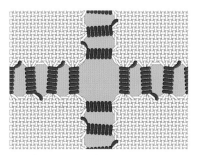

6 The completed cross intersection.

W3 variation

The blue line makes a W beside the intersection. The red line makes a 3 above and below the intersection.

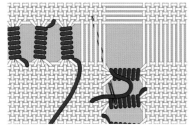

1 Work both lines of overcasting. Finish the blue line at the bottom, one bar before the intersection. Work the red line right up to the intersection, ending at the left. Bring the red thread out one thread further on from the unworked blue bar.

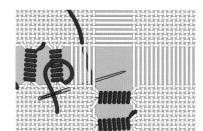

2 Pull the needle and thread through, and leave hanging for later use. Wrap the blue bar from bottom to top, treating the laced red thread as an extra thread to be overcast.

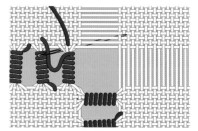

3 Finish the bar by sliding the needle under the bar and bringing it out one thread on from the far end of the adjacent bar, three threads up.

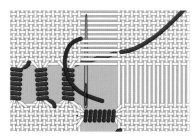

4 Pull the needle and blue thread through and leave it hanging for later use. Pull the red thread back through to the back. Bring it out in the drawn thread area, six threads away from the intersection. Work the first bar including the blue laced thread. Continue overcasting red bars.

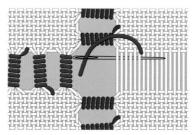

5 Pull the blue thread back through to the back. Bring it out in the drawn thread area, six threads away from the intersection, and continue overcasting bars in the blue line.

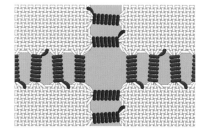

6 The completed cross intersection.

WE variation

The blue line makes a W beside the intersection. The red line makes an E above and below the intersection.

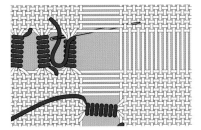

1 Work both lines of overcasting. Finish the red line on the left, one bar before the intersection. Work the blue line up to the intersection, ending at the top. Bring the blue thread out at the far side of the adjacent drawn thread area, two threads up and three right.

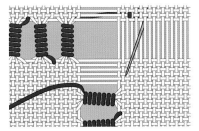

2 Pull the needle and thread through. Insert the needle one thread below. Bring it out in the drawn thread area, three threads to the right.

❶ *Use gentle tension, so that when the bar is wrapped, the blue thread does not become too tight.*

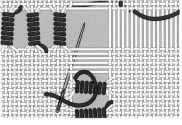

3 Pull the needle and thread through, and leave hanging for later use. Picking up the red thread, wrap the red bar from left to right.

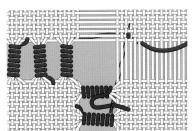

4 Finish the bar by sliding the needle under the bar and bringing it out three threads on from the far end of the adjacent bar, three threads across.

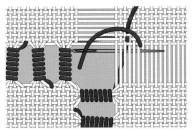

5 Pull the needle and thread through, and leave hanging for later use. Picking up the blue thread, work the next blue bar including the laced red thread. Continue overcasting bars in the blue line.

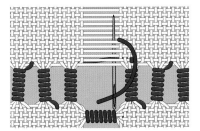

6 Pull the red thread back through to the back. Bring it out in the drawn thread area, six threads away from the intersection. Work the first bar including the laced blue thread. Continue overcasting bars in the red line.

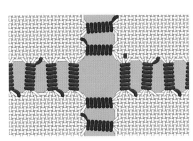

7 The completed cross intersection.

wiggly bars: t intersection – opening end

The two lines of overcast bars are shown in different colours for clarity. There are two variations of these intersections because of the way the wiggles meet.

M3 variation

The blue line makes an M beside the intersection. The red line makes a 3 above the intersection.

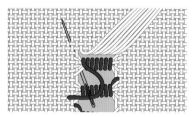

1 Having withdrawn the threads only to the end of the overcast bars, work up to the place where the intersection will begin, finishing on the left. Bring the needle out two threads left and two up from the gap above the overcast bar.

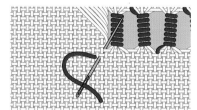

2 Pull the needle and thread through. Turn the work 90 degrees anticlockwise. Insert the needle one thread to the right, bringing it out again in the drawn thread area to the left of the final overcast bar.

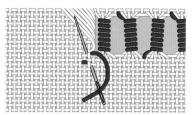

3 Pull the needle and thread through. Insert the needle three threads below. Bring it out three above and one left.
❶ *The short 'extra' stitch will be covered. It makes the first satin stitch sit properly, rather than just slipping around the corner from behind the overcast bar.*

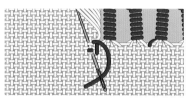

4 Pull the needle and thread through. Moving one thread left, work another satin stitch.

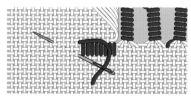

5 Work eight satin stitches. Insert the needle for the ninth stitch. Bring it out six threads left and three up, ready to begin the next overcast bar.

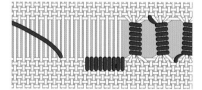

6 Pull the needle and thread through and leave them hanging for further use later. Withdraw the fabric threads further towards the left.

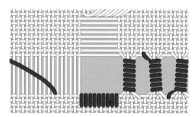

7 Carefully cut the threads on the inside edge of the satin stitch bar, and draw them back a little way.

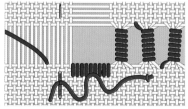

8 From the front, insert a new knotted thread below the centre of the next group of six threads, bringing it out just above the drawn thread area.

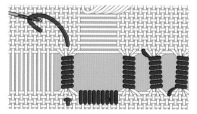

9 Pull the needle and thread through. Picking up the red thread, work the next red bar, including the laced blue thread.

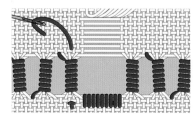

10 Continue on with the red overcast bars.

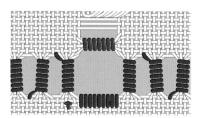

11 Pull the blue thread through to the back, and wrap the next blue overcast bar.

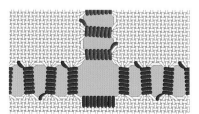

12 Continue working blue overcast bars. Cut off the knot at the beginning of the thread.

ME variation

The blue line makes an M beside the intersection. The red line makes an E above the intersection.

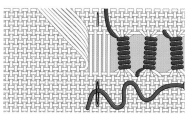

1 Withdraw the threads to where the intersection will start. Overcast to one bar away from this point, finishing at the top of the bar. From the front, insert a new knotted thread two threads below the centre of the next group of six threads, bringing it out two above the drawn thread area.

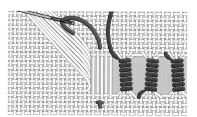

2 Pull the needle and blue thread through.

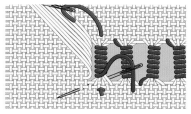

3 Treating the laced blue thread as another thread to be overcast, work another red overcast bar. Bring the needle out two threads left and two down from the gap left of the overcast bar.

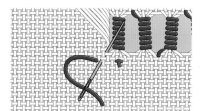

4 Pull the needle and thread through. Insert the needle one thread to the right, bringing it out again in the drawn thread area to the left of the final overcast bar.

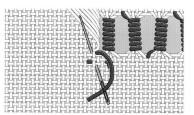

5 Pull the needle and thread through. Insert the needle three threads below. Bring it out three above and one left.
❶ *The short 'extra' stitch will be covered. It makes the first satin stitch sit properly, rather than just slipping around the corner from behind the overcast bar.*

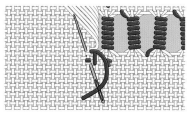

6 Pull the needle and thread through. Moving one thread left, work another satin stitch.

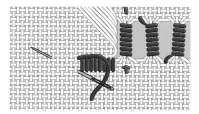

7 Work eight satin stitches. Insert the needle for the ninth stitch. Bring it out six threads left and three up, ready to begin the next overcast bar.

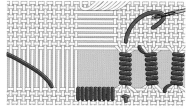

8 Pull the needle and thread through and leave them hanging for later use. Withdraw the fabric threads further left. Carefully cut the threads on the inside edge of the satin stitch bar, and draw them back a little way.

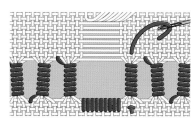

9 Continue overcasting bars in the red line.

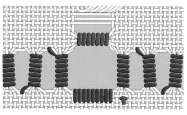

10 Pull the blue thread back through to the back, and wrap the next blue overcast bar.

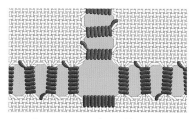

11 Continue working blue overcast bars. Cut off the knot at the beginning of the thread.

wiggly bars: t intersection – closing end

The two lines of overcast bars are shown in different colours for clarity. The blue line ends, and the red line continues. There are two variations because of the way the wiggles meet.

M3 variation

The red line makes a 3 above the intersection.
The blue line makes an M beside the intersection.

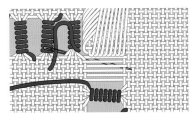

1 Withdraw the threads up to the intersection. Cease the red line one bar before the intersection, leaving the thread hanging for later use. Work the blue line up to the intersection, ending at the bottom. Bring the blue thread out one thread further on from the end of the adjacent unworked bar.

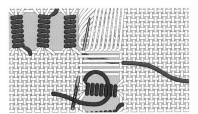

2 Pull the needle and blue thread through, and leave them hanging for later use. Insert the needle one thread left of the gap between bars. Bring the needle out in the intersection opening, treating the laced blue thread as an extra thread to be overcast.

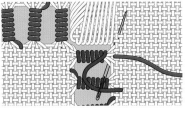

3 Overcast the bar from left to right, bringing the thread out again two threads right and up from the end of the drawn thread area.
❶ *Move the withdrawn threads out of the way if necessary.*

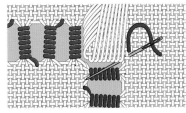

4 Insert the needle one thread below, bringing it out again in the drawn thread area beside the final overcast bar. Carefully trim the loose blue thread from the front of the fabric.

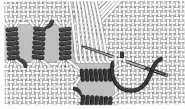

5 Pull the needle and thread through. Insert the needle three threads to the right, and bring it out again one above where it previously emerged.
❶ *The 'extra' stitch will be covered. It makes the first satin stitch sit properly, rather than just slipping around the corner from behind the overcast bar.*

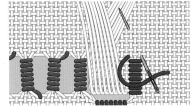

6 Work eight satin stitches. Insert the needle for the ninth stitch. Bring it out six threads up and three left, ready to begin the next overcast bar.

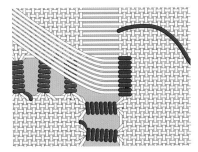

7 Pull the needle and thread through and leave them hanging for further use later. Withdraw the vertical fabric threads further upwards.

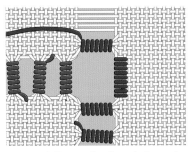

8 Carefully cut the threads from the inside edge of the satin stitch. Remove them. Overcast the next bar from right to left.

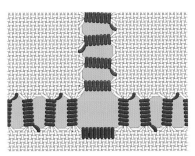

9 Continue on with the red overcast bars. Turn the work 90 degrees clockwise to view it as an M3 intersection.

ME variation

The blue line makes an M beside the intersection.

The red line makes an E above the intersection.

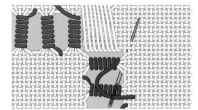

1 Withdraw the threads up to the intersection. Work the blue line up to the intersection, ending at the top. Work the red line up to the intersection, with the final bar from left to right. Bring the thread out again two threads right and up from the end of the drawn thread area.

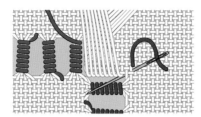

2 Insert the needle one thread below, bringing it out again in the drawn thread area above the final overcast bar.

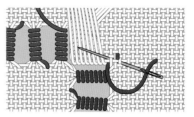

3 Pull the needle and thread through. Insert the needle three threads to the right, and bring it out again one above where it previously emerged.

❶ *The 'extra' stitch will be covered. It makes the first satin stitch sit properly, rather than just slipping around the corner from behind the overcast bar.*

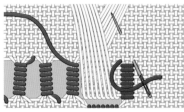

4 Work eight satin stitches. Insert the needle for the ninth stitch. Bring it out six threads up and three left, ready to begin the next overcast bar.

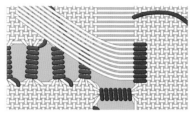

5 Pull the needle and thread through and leave them hanging for further use later. Withdraw the vertical fabric threads further upwards.

6 Carefully cut the threads from the inside edge of the satin stitch. Remove them. Picking up the blue thread, finish the bar and bring the blue thread out one thread further on from the centre of the adjacent unworked bar.

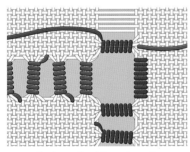

7 Including the blue thread, overcast the first red bar from right to left. Carefully trim the loose blue thread from the front of the fabric.

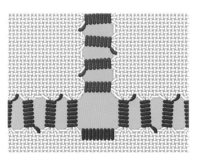

8 Continue on with the red overcast bars. Turn the work 90 degrees clockwise to view it as an M3 intersection.

W3 variation

The red line makes a 3 above the intersection. The blue line makes a W beside the intersection.

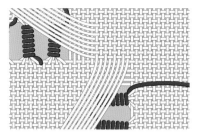

1 Withdraw the threads up to the intersection. Work both lines to one bar before it, with the blue finishing at the top, and the red at the right.

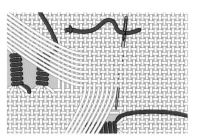

2 Insert a needle with a knotted new blue thread, one thread up and right from the intersection. Bring it out one thread left and nine down.

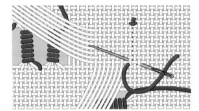

3 Pull the needle and thread through. Insert the needle three threads right, and bring it out one above where it previously emerged.
❶ *Catch the blue thread in at the back.*

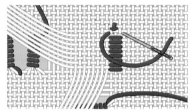

4 Pull the needle and thread through. Work eight satin stitches. Insert the needle for the ninth stitch. Finish the thread by running it under the back of the satin stitch.

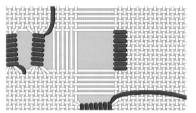

5 Withdraw the vertical threads further upwards. Cut the threads from the inside edge of the satin stitch. Remove them. Carefully cut off the blue knot.

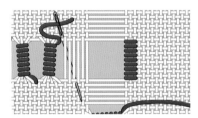

6 Pick up the blue thread and insert the needle one thread above. Bring the needle out one thread on from the far side of the unwrapped blue bar.

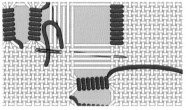

7 Pull the needle and thread through. Insert the needle one thread below. Bring the needle out one thread on from the far side of the unwrapped red bar.
❶ *Use gentle tension for the laced threads.*

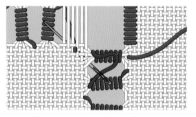

8 Pull the blue thread through. Picking up the red thread, work the unwrapped bar in the red line including the laced thread, then take the needle behind the fabric and bring it out ready to start the next bar in the blue line.

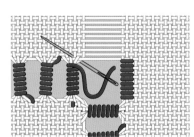

9 Carefully trim the end of the blue thread. Continuing with the red thread, overcast the last bar in the blue line, including the laced thread. Finish the bar and bring the needle out one thread above the centre of the bar.

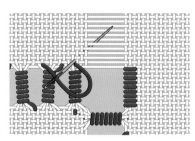

10 Insert the needle one thread above, and bring it out in the red line, six threads up from the intersection.

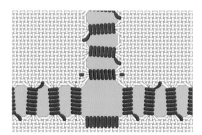

11 Continue working red bars as before. Turn the work 90 degrees clockwise to view it as a W3 intersection.

WE variation

The red line makes an E above the intersection. The blue line makes a W beside the intersection.

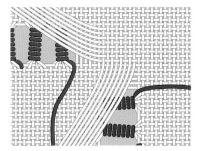

1 Withdraw the threads up to the intersection. Work both lines to one bar before it, with the blue finishing at the bottom, and the red at the right.

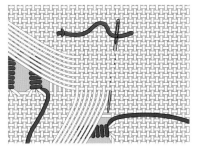

2 Insert a needle with a knotted new blue thread, one thread up and right from the intersection. Bring it out one thread left and nine down.

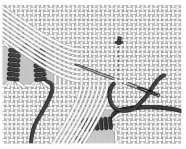

3 Pull the needle and thread through. Insert the needle three threads right, and bring it out one above where it previously emerged.
❶ *Catch the blue thread in at the back.*

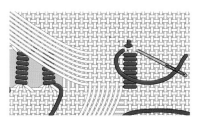

4 Pull the needle and thread through. Work eight satin stitches. Insert the needle for the ninth stitch. Finish the thread by running it under the back of the satin stitch.

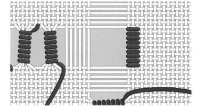

5 Withdraw the vertical threads further upwards. Cut the threads from the inside edge of the satin stitch. Remove them. Carefully cut off the blue knot.

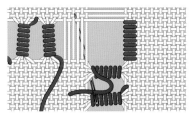

6 Pick up the red thread, and work the unwrapped bar in the red line, then take the needle behind the fabric and bring it out one thread further on from the end of the unwrapped blue bar.

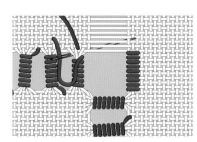

7 Pull the red thread through and leave for later use. Pick up the blue thread and overcast the bar, including the laced red thread. Finish the bar and bring the needle out one thread further on from the end of the next red bar.

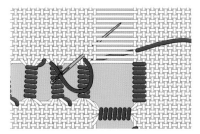

8 Pull the needle and blue thread through. Pick up the red thread and insert the needle one thread above, bringing it out in the red line, six threads up from the intersection.

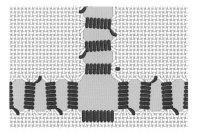

9 Work the first bar including the laced blue thread. Continue working red bars as before. Carefully trim the end of the blue thread. Turn the work 90 degrees clockwise to view it as a W3 intersection.

wiggly bars: t bar intersection – opening end

There are four variations of these intersections because of the way the wiggles meet.

SW variation

The two lines of overcast bars are shown in different colours for clarity. The blue line makes a W beside the intersection. The red line makes an S through the intersection.

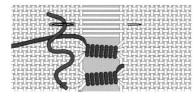

1 Work up to and including the bar that will sit in the centre of the intersection, finishing on the left. Leave the thread hanging for later use. From the front, insert a new blue knotted thread two threads left of the centre of the next group of six, bringing it out on the drawn thread area's far side.

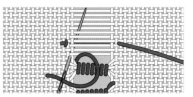

2 Pull the needle and blue thread through. Leave the thread hanging for later use. Continue on overcasting the next red bar from left to right, treating the laced blue thread as an extra thread to be overcast.

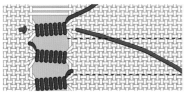

3 Leave the thread for later use.
❶ *The dotted lines show the new drawn thread area. The horizontal threads within will be cut, drawn back to the left, then overcast into the first blue bar, to secure them properly.*

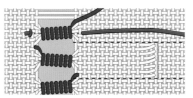

4 Cut the threads in the new drawn thread area, about 20 threads right of the red line of bars. Start drawing them back to the left.

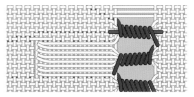

5 Turn the work over to the back and draw the threads right back to the red bars.

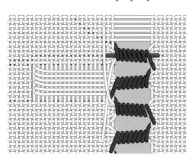

6 Take the top withdrawn thread and fold it down to lay parallel with the red line of bars. Take the bottom thread and fold it up to lay parallel, crossing the other folded thread.

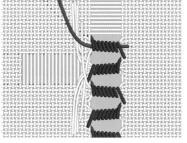

7 Of the six remaining withdrawn threads, fold the top three up, and the bottom three down. Pull the loose end of the blue thread through to the back.
❶ *The threads can be pinned in place.*

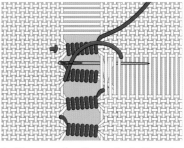

8 Turn to the front. Including the extra threads on the back, tightly wrap the first blue bar over five fabric threads only, so it is not much thicker than the others. Work half the stitches above and below the central red bar.

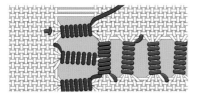

9 Working over six threads, continue overcasting bars in the blue line.

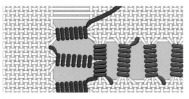

10 Trim the thread ends on the back, and the blue knot from the front.

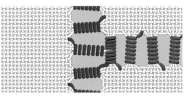

11 Continue overcasting bars in the red line.

ZM variation

The two lines of overcast bars are shown in different colours for clarity. The blue line makes an M beside the intersection. The red line makes a Z through the intersection.

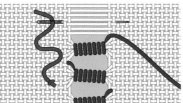

1 Work red bars, finishing on the right one unwrapped bar below the intersection. Leave the thread hanging for later use. From the front, insert a new blue knotted thread two threads left of the centre of the next group of six, bringing it out on the far side of the drawn thread area.

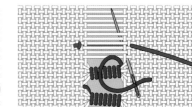

2 Pull the needle and blue thread through. Leave the thread hanging for later use. Continue on overcasting the next red bar from right to left, treating the laced blue thread as an extra thread to be overcast.

3 Wrap two more bars, ending on the left. Leave the thread for later use.
❶ *The dotted lines show the new drawn thread area. The horizontal threads within will be cut, drawn back to the left, then overcast into the first blue bar, to secure them properly.*

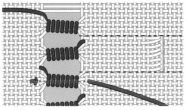

4 Cut the threads in the new drawn thread area, about 20 threads right of the red line of bars. Start drawing them back to the left.

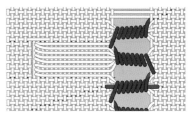

5 Turn the work over to the back and draw the threads right back to the red bars.

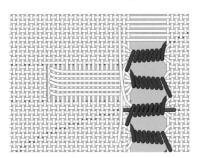

6 Take the top withdrawn thread and fold it down to lay parallel with the red line of bars. Take the bottom thread and fold it up to lay parallel, crossing the other folded thread.

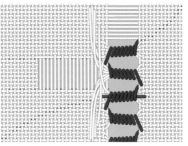

7 Of the six remaining withdrawn threads, fold the top three up, and the bottom three down. Pull the loose end of the blue thread through to the back.
❶ *The threads can be pinned in place.*

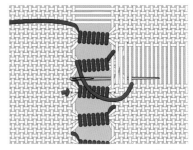

8 Turn over to the front. Including the laced threads, tightly wrap the first blue bar over five fabric threads only, so it is not much thicker than the others. Work half the stitches below and half above the central red bar.

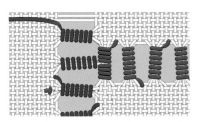

9 Working over six fabric threads, keep wrapping bars in the blue line.

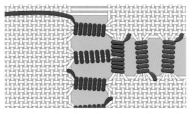

10 Trim the thread ends on the back, and the blue knot from the front.

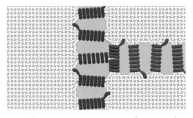

11 Continue overcasting bars in the red line.

71

wiggly bars: t bar intersection – closing end

There are four variations of these intersections because of the way the wiggles meet.

MS variation

The two lines of overcast bars are shown in different colours for clarity. The blue line makes an M beside the intersection. The red line makes an S through the intersection.

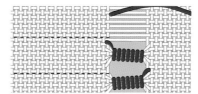

1 Work the red bars up to and including the one sitting in the intersection, finishing on the left. Bring the thread out ready to start the next bar, and leave it hanging for later use.

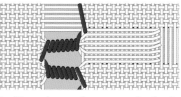

2 Turn the work over to the back. Draw back the cut horizontal threads to one thread before the red bar.
❶ *Do not trim the withdrawn threads.*

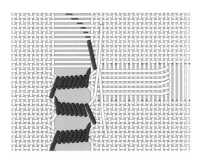

3 Take the top withdrawn thread and fold it down to lay parallel with the red line of bars. Take the bottom thread and fold it up to lay parallel, crossing the other folded thread.

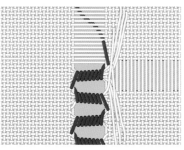

4 Of the six remaining withdrawn threads, fold the top three up, and the bottom three down.
❶ *The threads can be pinned in place.*

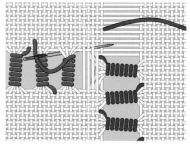

5 On the front, work the blue line up to the bar (of five fabric threads only) before the intersection, ending at the top. Bring the needle out one thread up and three to the right from the gap between the two bars.

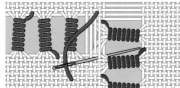

6 Pull the needle and thread through. Insert the needle at the far end of the bar, one thread down. Bring it out between the last two red bars.

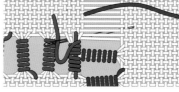

7 Pull the needle and thread through. Overcast the bar tightly so that it is not much thicker than the others. Work stitches on either side of the central red bar. Bring the needle out on the far side of the next red bar.

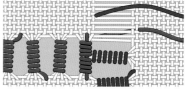

8 Pull the needle and thread through and leave them hanging for further use later. Trim the thread ends on the back.

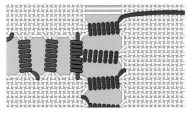

9 With the red thread, overcast the next red bar from left to right, including the laced blue thread. Trim the end of the blue thread.

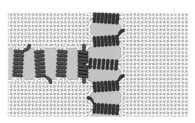

10 Continue stitching red bars as before.

WZ variation

The two lines of overcast bars are shown in different colours for clarity. The blue line makes a W beside the intersection. The red line makes a Z through the intersection.

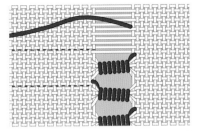

1 Work the red bars up to and including the one sitting in the intersection, finishing on the right. Bring the thread out ready to start the next bar, and leave it hanging for later use.

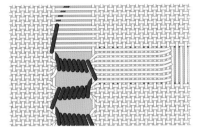

2 Turn the work over to the back. Draw back the cut horizontal threads to one thread before the red bar.
❶ *Do not trim the withdrawn threads.*

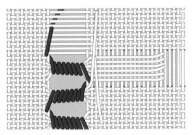

3 Take the top withdrawn thread and fold it down to lay parallel with the red line of bars. Take the bottom thread and fold it up to lay parallel, crossing the other folded thread.

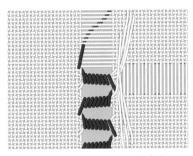

4 Of the six remaining withdrawn threads, fold the top three up, and the bottom three down.
❶ *The threads can be pinned in place.*

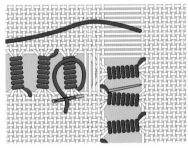

5 On the front, work the blue line up to the bar (of five fabric threads only) before the intersection, ending at the bottom. Insert the needle one thread below the gap after the blue bar. Bring it out again between the last two red bars.

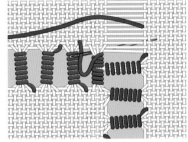

6 Pull the needle and thread through. Including all the withdrawn threads on the back, overcast the bar tightly so that it is not much thicker than the others. Work half the stitches below and half above the central red bar. Bring the needle out on the far side of the next red bar to be overcast.

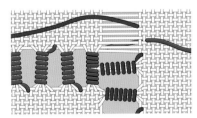

7 Pull the needle and thread through and leave them hanging for further use later. Trim the thread ends on the back.

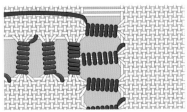

8 Overcast the next red bar from right to left, treating the laced blue thread as an extra thread to be overcast. Trim the end of the blue thread.

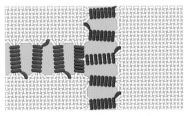

9 Continue stitching red bars as before.

zigzag overcast bars

Whereas the other methods of overcasting bars are worked over groups of six threads, this method uses groups of four.

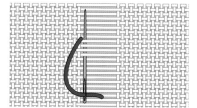

1 Remove eight threads from the fabric to create the drawn thread area. Bring the needle out at the left side of the drawn thread area, at the top of the first group of four threads. From below, slide the needle under the four threads.

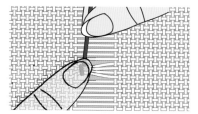

2 Pull the needle through. To tighten the stitch, pinch the stitch between your forefinger and thumb, and pull the thread away from it with the other hand.

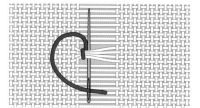

3 A little to the right, slide the needle under the same four threads, from below.

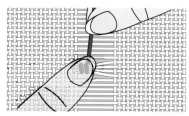

4 Make sure the new stitch sits next to the previous one, rather than on top of it, and then pinch and pull to tighten.

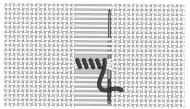

5 Work the remainder of the bar in the same way, ensuring tension remains consistent. To tie this bar to the next one, from below, slide the needle under the bar and the four threads above it.

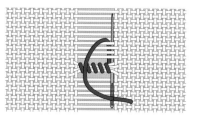

6 Slide the needle under the bar and four threads above again.

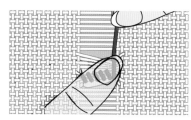

7 Pinch and pull to tighten, bringing the ends of the bars close together.

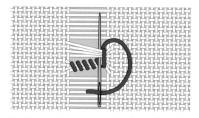

8 From below and a little to the left, slide the needle under the new bar.

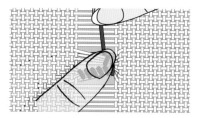

9 Pinch and pull to tighten.

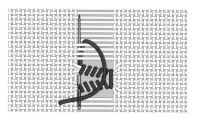

10 Moving left, wrap the rest of the bar with consistent tension. To tie this bar to the next one, from below, slide the needle under the bar and the four threads above it.

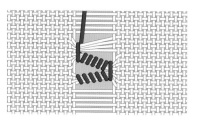

11 Slide the needle under the bar and four threads above again. Then pinch and pull to tighten, bringing the bar ends close together.

12 Continue zigzagging back and forth across the bars to fill the drawn thread area.

❶ *For consistency, all bars should have the same quantity of wraps.*

74

zigzag bars: turning a corner

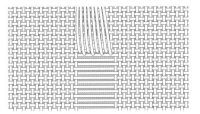

1 Withdraw the threads to where the overcast bars will end.

❶ *This will mean that the fabric remains intact for sewing the satin stitch bars. If the threads were withdrawn further, it would be less stable and harder to stitch.*

2 Stitch up to the corner. To finish the final bar, slide the needle under the bar, bringing the needle out two threads left and up from the top of the last group of four threads.

❶ *The last bar will need to finish on the left.*

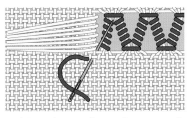

3 Turn the work 90 degrees anti-clockwise. Pull the needle through. Insert it one thread to the right. Bring it out in the drawn thread area to the left of the last overcast bar.

❶ *This little stitch will be covered by the satin stitch bar. It makes the end of the satin stitch bar sit more neatly.*

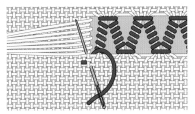

4 Insert the needle three threads below, bringing it out again one thread left of where the thread last emerged.

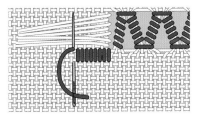

5 Complete a satin stitch bar of nine stitches. To finish the bar and start the next, bring the needle out in the same hole again.

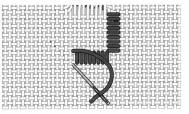

6 Turn the work 90 degrees anti-clockwise, and move the withdrawn thread ends out of the way. Stitch a bar of nine satin stitches for the other side of the corner. Take the thread to the back of the fabric.

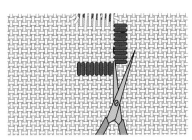

7 Cut the eight fabric threads on the inside edge of each satin stitch bar.

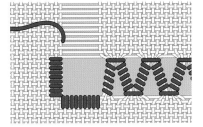

8 Turn the work 90 degrees clock-wise. Remove the old threads, and draw back the newly cut ones for the new line of stitching. Bring the needle out four threads up in the drawn thread area, to begin the new bar.

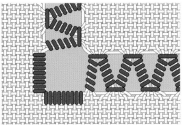

9 Continue stitching overcast bars in the same way as before.

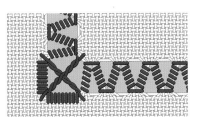

❶ *Corners can also be worked with a cross filling. See p76.*

cross filling

Shown worked in a corner here, this filling can be worked in any type of intersection.

The threads for the corner or intersection must be cut and withdrawn before working cross fillings.

The first half of the cross should be worked after the third side of the square (whether overcast bars or satin stitch bars); the second half after the fourth side.

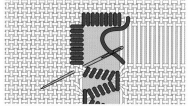

1 Work the satin stitch corner bars. Cut and withdraw the threads. Bring the needle out two threads up and right from the top right corner of the intersection. Insert it under the far corner, bringing it out two threads down and left from the corner.

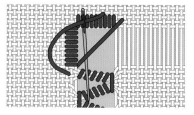

2 Pull the needle and thread through. Slide the needle under the first stitch, from above.

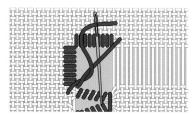

3 Pull the needle and thread so that the threads gently intertwine. Slide the needle under the first stitch again, from above.

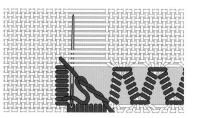

4 Turn the work 90 degrees anticlockwise. Slide the needle under the crossing thread, from below. Bring the needle to the front after the four threads for the new overcast bar.

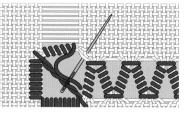

5 Pull the needle and thread so the threads intertwine. Work the first bar on the new side. Bring the needle out two threads up and right from the top right corner of the intersection.

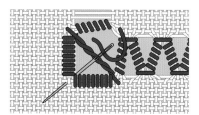

6 Pull the needle and thread through. Take the needle over the first half of the cross, and insert it under the far corner, bringing it out two threads down and left from the corner.

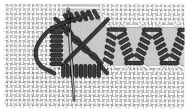

7 Pull the needle and thread through. Slide the needle under the most recent crossing stitch, from above.

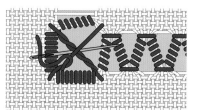

8 Pull the needle and thread through. Slide the needle under all the crossed threads, in the centre, from left to right.

9 Pull the needle and thread through, tightening so the threads intertwine. Above the cross, slide the needle under the top half of the most recent crossing stitch from left to right.

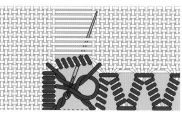

10 Pull the needle and thread through, so the threads intertwine. Slide the needle under the first bar of the new side and the next four threads, ready to continue.

11 Continue working bars as before.

zigzag bars: cross intersection

M3 variation

The blue line makes an M beside the intersection. The red line makes a 3 above and below the intersection.

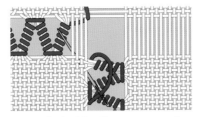

1 Work the blue line up to one bar from the intersection, finishing at the top. Bring the blue thread out in the intersection. Work the last bar of the red line before the intersection, finishing at the left. Take the needle to the far side of the last four threads in the blue line.

2 Wrap the final bar of the blue line with the red thread, finishing with the thread ready for the next bar in the red line. Picking up the blue thread insert the needle left of the last two bars, bringing it out two threads above the gap between the two bars.

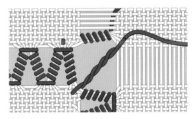

3 Pull the needle and thread through. Insert the needle one thread below. Bring it out again two threads further on from the end of the unwrapped red bar.

4 Pull the needle and thread through and leave it hanging for later use. Picking up the red thread, wrap the next red bar, including the laced blue thread. Bring the thread out ready to begin the next bar.

❶ *If working the cross filling, use the blue thread to work the first half of the cross from top right to bottom left, following the cross filling instructions on p76.*

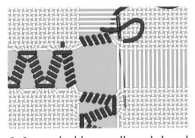

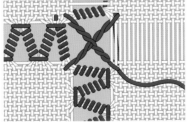

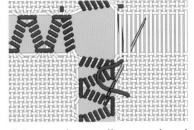

5 Insert the blue needle and thread one thread to the left, bringing it out two threads on from the far side of the next unwrapped blue bar.

❶ *If working the cross filling, use the blue thread to complete the cross from bottom right to top left, following the cross filling instructions on p76.*

6 Insert the needle one thread below, bringing the needle out in the drawn thread area after the four threads to be used for the next bar.

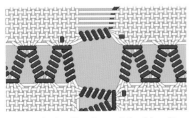

7 Work the first bar of the blue line including the laced thread. Continue as before, working bars in the blue line.

8 Continue working bars in the red line.

❶ *The completed intersection with cross filling.*

The blue line makes an M beside the intersection. The red line makes an E above and below the intersection.

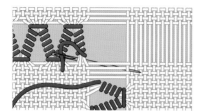

1 Work the red line, stopping at the left, one bar before the intersection. Work the blue line up to the intersection, finishing at the bottom. Bring the needle out one thread on from the far end of the next red bar.

2 Pull the needle and blue thread through. Picking up the red thread, finish the bar, and take the needle behind the laced thread and the final two bars.

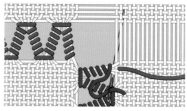

3 Work the red bar including the laced thread. Bring the needle out two threads on from the far end of the next blue bar.

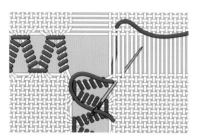

4 Pull the needle and red thread through. Picking up the blue thread, insert it one thread right of where it emerged. Bring it out in the drawn thread area after the first four threads.

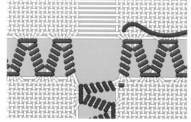

5 Pull the needle through. Work the first blue bar, including the laced red thread. Continue on, working blue bars.

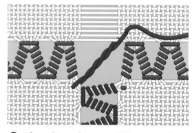

❶ *If working the cross filling, use the red thread to work the first half of the cross from top right to bottom left, following the cross filling instructions on p76.*

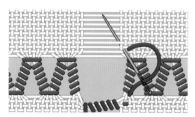

6 Insert the needle and red thread one thread to the left. Bring it out in the drawn thread area, after the four threads for the next red bar.

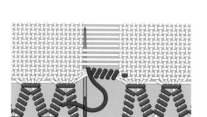

7 Work the red bar and finish by bringing the needle out four threads above, ready to wrap the first and second bars together.

❶ *If working the cross filling, instead of finishing up four threads above, insert the needle under the threads at the top left corner of the intersection, bringing it out two threads up and left.*

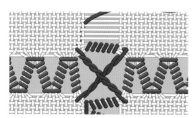

❶ *Work the second half of the cross filling from top left to bottom right. Finish by bringing the thread out four threads above the red bar, ready to wrap the first and second bars together.*

8 Continue working bars in the red line.

❶ *The completed intersection with cross filling.*

The blue line makes a W beside the intersection. The red line makes a 3 above and below the intersection.

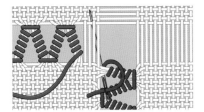

1 Work the blue line stopping at the bottom, one bar from the intersection. Work the last bar of the red line before the intersection, finishing on the left. Bring the needle out at the far side of the last unwrapped bar in the blue line, one thread up.

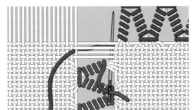

2 Pull the needle and red thread through. Turn the work 90 degrees anticlockwise. Picking up the blue thread, take the needle under the laced red thread and the final two bars.

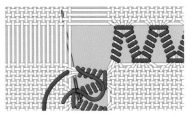

3 Wrap the two bars together at the right end, and work the blue bar, including the laced red thread. Finish the bar and bring the needle out two threads on from the far end of the next red bar.

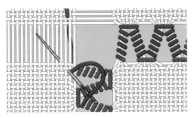

4 Pull the needle and blue thread through. Insert the needle and red thread one thread to the left. Bring it out in the drawn thread area after the first four threads in the red line.

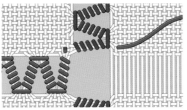

5 Turn the work 90 degrees clockwise. Overcast the first bar, including the laced blue thread. Continue working bars in the red line as before.

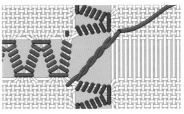

❶ *If working the cross filling, use the blue thread to work the first half of the cross from top right to bottom left, following the cross filling instructions on p76.*

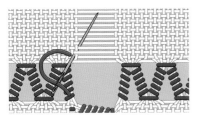

6 Turn the work 90 degrees anticlockwise. Insert the needle and blue thread one thread to the right. Bring it out in the drawn thread area, ready to work the next blue bar.

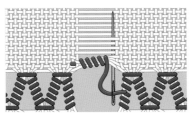

7 Work the first bar, taking the needle under the bar and the next four threads, ready to wrap the two bars together.

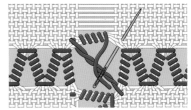

❶ *If working the cross filling, instead of bringing the needle out as in Step 7, bring the needle out in the top right corner of the intersection, two threads right and up.*

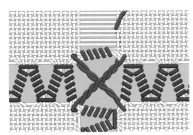

❶ *Work the second half of the cross filling, from top right to bottom left, referring to the cross filling instructions on p76.*

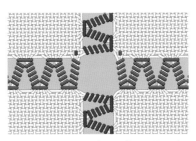

8 Continue working bars in the blue line to complete the intersection.

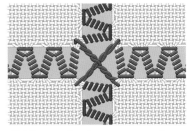

❶ *The completed intersection with cross filling.*

WE variation

The blue line makes a W beside the intersection. The red line makes an E above and below the intersection.

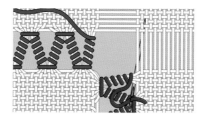

1 Work the blue line up to the intersection, finishing at the top. With the red thread, work the bar before the intersection, finishing on the right. Bring the needle out at the far side of the next bar in the blue line, two threads up.

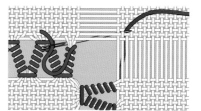

2 Pull the needle and red thread through. Picking up the blue thread, bring the needle out at the far side of the next bar in the red line, two threads to the right.

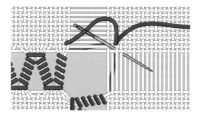

3 Insert the needle and blue thread one thread below, bringing it out in the drawn thread area, two threads to the right.

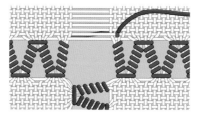

4 Work the first bar in the blue line, including the laced red thread. Continue working bars in the blue line.

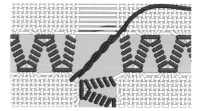

❶ *If working the cross filling, use the red thread to work the first half of the cross from top right to bottom left, following the cross filling instructions on p76.*

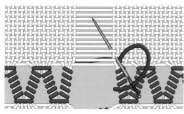

5 Insert the needle and red thread one thread to the left, bringing the needle out in the drawn thread area, two threads above.

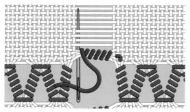

6 Work the red bar, including the blue laced thread. To finish, take the needle behind the bar and the four threads above, ready to wrap the two bars together.

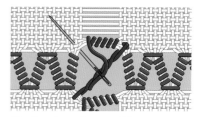

❶ *If working the cross filling, instead of bringing the needle out as in Step 6, bring the needle out in the top left corner of the intersection, two threads left and up.*

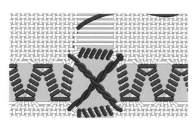

❶ *Work the second half of the cross filling, from top left to bottom right, referring to the cross filling instructions on p76.*

7 Continue working bars in the red line to complete the intersection.

❶ *The completed intersection with cross filling.*

zigzag bars: t intersection – opening end

The two lines of overcast bars are shown in different colours for clarity. There are two variations of each of these intersections because of the way the zigzags meet.

M3 variation

The blue line makes an M beside the intersection.
The red line makes a 3 above the intersection.

1 Withdraw the threads up to the intersection. Work bars right up to the intersection, finishing at the bottom. Bring the needle out two threads left and down from the gap after the final bar.

2 Pull the needle and thread through. Insert the needle one thread to the right, bringing it out again in the drawn thread area to the left of the final bar.

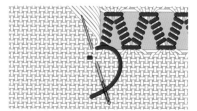

3 Pull the needle and thread through. Insert the needle three threads below. Bring it out three up and one left.

❶ *This little stitch will be covered by the satin stitch bar. It makes the end of the satin stitch bar sit more neatly.*

4 Pull the needle and thread through. Moving left by one thread each time, work eight satin stitches. Insert the needle for the ninth stitch. Bring it out four threads left and three up. Withdraw the threads further left.

5 Turn the work 90 degrees clockwise. Cut and draw back the threads on the satin stitch's inside edge. From the front, insert a knotted thread two to left of the next bar. Bring it out two threads right of the drawn thread area.

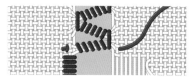

6 Pull the needle and blue thread through. Work the first red bar, including the blue laced thread. Continue overcasting bars in the red line.

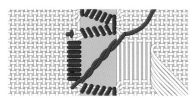

❶ *If working the cross filling, use the blue thread to work the first half from top right to bottom left, following the cross filling instructions on p76.*

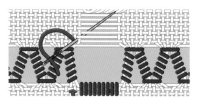

7 Turn the work 90 degrees anti-clockwise. Insert the needle one thread to the right, bringing it out in the drawn thread area after the first four threads of the new blue line.

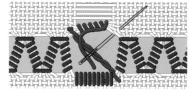

❶ *If working the cross filling, work the blue bar and bring the needle out in the top right corner of the intersection, two threads right and up.*

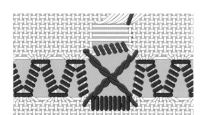

❶ *Work the second half of the cross filling from top left to bottom right, with the cross filling instructions on p76.*

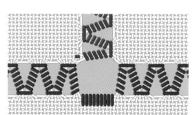

8 Continue by working bars in the blue line. After stitching the first blue bar, the knot can be cut off.

❶ *The completed intersection with cross filling.*

ME variation

The blue line makes an M beside the intersection. The red line makes an E above the intersection.

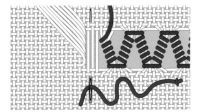

1 Withdraw the threads up to the intersection. Work bars, stopping one bar before the intersection, finishing at the top. From the front, insert a new knotted thread two threads below the last bar, bringing it out two above the drawn thread area.

2 Pull the needle and blue thread through. Work the final red bar, including the blue laced thread. Finish the bar and bring the needle out two threads left and down from the gap after the final bar.

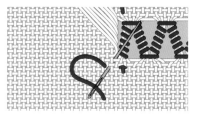

3 Pull the needle and thread through. Insert the needle one thread to the right, bringing it out again in the drawn thread area to the left of the final bar.

4 Pull the needle and thread through. Insert the needle three threads below. Bring it out three up and one left.
❶ *This little stitch will be covered by the satin stitch bar. It makes the end of the satin stitch bar sit more neatly.*

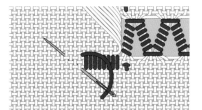

5 Pull the needle and thread through. Continuing to move left by one thread each time, work eight satin stitches. Insert the needle for the ninth stitch. Bring it out four threads left and three up.

6 Withdraw the threads further to the left. Cut the threads on the inside edge of the satin stitch bar and draw the threads back a little way. Continue overcasting bars in the red line.

❶ *If working the cross filling, use the blue thread to work the first half from top right to bottom left, following the cross filling instructions on p76.*

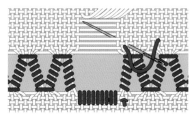

7 Insert the needle and blue thread one thread to the right, bringing it out in the drawn thread area after the first four threads of the new blue line.

❶ *If working the cross filling, work the blue bar. Bring the needle out in the top left corner of the intersection, two threads left and up. Carefully cut off the blue knot.*

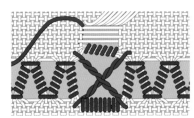

❶ *Work the second half of the cross filling, from top left to bottom right, referring to the cross filling instructions on p76.*

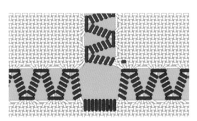

8 Work bars in the blue line as before, to complete the intersection. After stitching the first blue bar, the knot can be trimmed off.

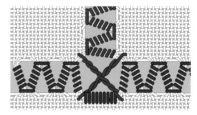

❶ *The completed intersection with cross filling.*

zigzag bars: t intersection – closing end

The two lines of overcast bars are shown in different colours for clarity. There are two variations of each of these interesections because of the way the zigzags meet.

M3 variation

The blue line makes an M beside the intersection.
The red line makes a 3 above the intersection.

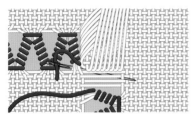

1 Withdraw the threads up to the intersection. Stop the red line one bar before it, ending on the left. Finish the line of blue bars at the bottom. Bring the needle out one thread on from the far end of the next red bar.

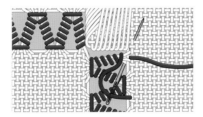

2 Picking up the red thread, work the last bar of the red line before the intersection, including the blue laced thread. Bring the needle out two threads right and up from the drawn thread area after the last bar.

3 Insert the needle one thread below, bringing it out again in the drawn thread area above the final overcast bar. Carefully trim the loose blue thread from the front of the fabric.

4 Pull the needle through. Insert it three threads to the right. Bring it out one above where it previously emerged.
❶ *This little stitch will be covered by the satin stitch bar. It makes the end of the satin stitch bar sit more neatly.*

5 Work eight satin stitches. Insert the needle for the ninth stitch, and take the thread to the back.

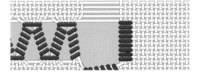

6 Withdraw the vertical threads further upwards. Cut the threads from the inside edge of the satin stitch. Remove them.

❶ *If working the cross filling, work the first half from top right to bottom left, using the cross filling instructions on p76.*

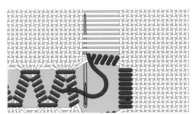

7 Work the next bar and take the needle behind the bar and the four threads above, ready to wrap the two bars together.

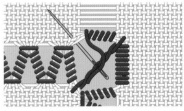

❶ *If working the cross filling, instead of bringing the needle out as in Step 7, bring it out in the top left corner of the intersection, two threads left and up.*

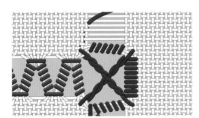

❶ *Work the second half of the cross filling from top left to bottom right, using the instructions on p76.*

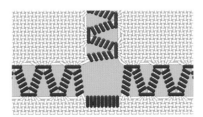

8 Turn the work 90 degrees clockwise. Continue working bars in the red line to complete the intersection.

❶ *The completed intersection with cross filling.*

ME variation

The blue line makes an M beside the intersection. The red line makes an E above the intersection.

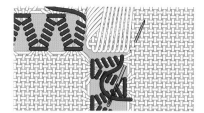

1 Work the blue line up to the intersection, finishing at the top. With the red thread, work the bar before the intersection, finishing on the right. Bring the needle out two threads right and up from the drawn thread area after the last bar.

2 Insert the needle one thread below, bringing it out again in the drawn thread area above the final overcast bar.

3 Pull the needle through. Insert it three threads to the right. Bring it out one above where it previously emerged.

❶ *This little stitch will be covered by the satin stitch bar. It makes the end of the satin stitch bar sit more neatly.*

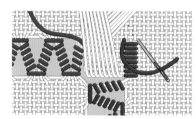

4 Work eight satin stitches. Insert the needle for the ninth stitch, and take the thread to the back.

5 Withdraw the vertical threads further upwards. Cut the threads from the inside edge of the satin stitch. Remove them. Picking up the blue thread, bring the needle out at the far side of the next bar in the red line, one thread to the right.

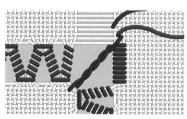

❶ *If working the cross filling, use the red thread to work the first half from top right to bottom left, following the cross filling instructions on p76.*

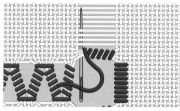

6 With the red thread, work the first bar, including the blue laced thread. Take the needle behind the bar and the four threads above, ready to wrap the two bars together. Trim the end of the blue thread.

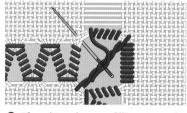

❶ *If working the cross filling, instead of bringing the needle out as in Step 6, bring it out in the top left corner of the intersection, two threads left and up.*

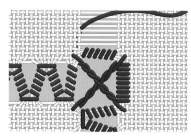

❶ *Work the second half of the cross filling from top left to bottom right, using the instructions on p76.*

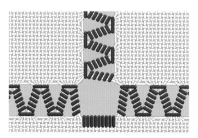

7 Turn the work 90 degrees clockwise. Continue working bars in the red line to complete the intersection.

❶ *The completed intersection with cross filling.*

surface embroidery

When the drawn thread work is complete, the surface embroidery is stitched. A profusion of bullions and eyelets create a sumptuous surface of texture and pattern.

tracing patterns

Individually trace the motif for each panel, centring the fabric over the pattern for each square or rectangle.

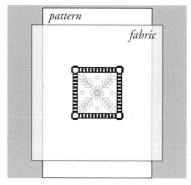

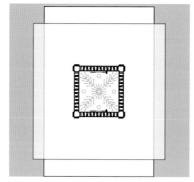

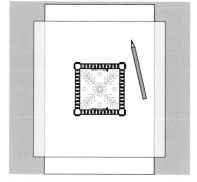

1 Centre the freshly ironed fabric over the pattern for each square or rectangle.

❶ *Tracing each motif separately leads to better accuracy.*

❶ *Using a lightbox or holding the fabric and pattern up to a lighted window makes the process much easier.*

2 Pin the pattern in place at the edge of the panel to be traced, so there is no chance it will move during tracing.

3 Using a wash-out pencil or an HB pencil with a very light touch, trace the pattern onto the fabric.

❶ *You will need to cover the markings with stitching or be able to wash them out, so do not make them very dark and heavy.*

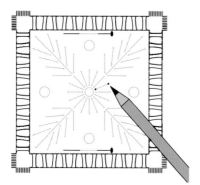

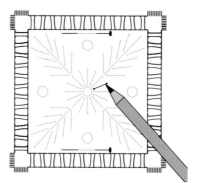

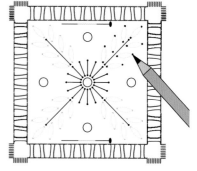

4 Mark the end of each line with a dot…

5 …then draw the line between the end dots.

❶ *The end dots mean that the end points of the line are clearly visible, enabling better accuracy of stitch length.*

❶ *For double bullions (shown in pink lines on the pattern), just mark the end dots, but not the lines, because your bullions may curve differently than what is drawn on the pattern.*

starting threads

There are a number of methods for starting a new thread. Never carry threads over long distances on the back of the work. This can pucker and be prone to snagging, or show through obviously from the front. Finish the thread and start anew.

under existing stitching

When there is already existing stitching nearby, you can anchor the thread in the back of that stitching.

1 On the back of the fabric, run the thread under the nearby stitching.

2 Take a small backstitch or two and continue under the stitching.

3 Take the thread to the front at the desired location and begin stitching.

split back stitch

This method creates a firm, easily coverable start.

1 On the front, bring the thread out where it will be covered by stitching. Take a very short stitch. Pull the thread nearly all the way through, leaving just a very short tail.

❶ *Alternatively, use a knot and cut it off once the backstitching is complete.*

2 Insert the needle between the tail and where the thread emerged, thereby piercing the stitch on the back of the fabric.

❶ *If it pulls the thread end through to the back a little more, that is fine. It will probably completely disappear later.*

3 Bring the needle up a little further on. Insert the needle into the back-stitch, piercing it.

❶ *This will securely anchor the thread, and can now be stitched over.*

waste knot

This method works well in places where there is no existing stitching.

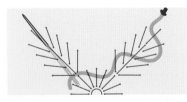

1 Make a knot in the end of the thread. From the front of the fabric, enter the needle about 8cm (3in) away from the start of the stitching.

2 Begin stitching. When there is enough stitching to run the thread under, cut off the knot. Rethread the thread into a needle.

3 On the back of the fabric, run the thread under the back of the stitching. A back stitch can help to further anchor it. Trim any excess thread.

finishing threads

To finish a thread, take it through to the back and run it under the back of the stitching, adding a few back stitches to help secure the thread.

bullion knot

Canutilho

Bullion stitch is one of the most important stitches in Guimarães embroidery.

1 Use a straw needle. Bring the thread out of the fabric. Insert the needle again some distance away.

❶ *A straw needle has a narrow eye which slides through the wraps easier.*

3 With gentle tension, wrap the thread around the needle three times in a clockwise direction.

❶ *If you wrap too tightly, you will only make it harder to pull your needle through. However, if you wrap too loosely, there is more likelihood that the wraps will be messed up as you pull the needle through.*

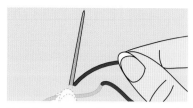

2 Bring the needle out where the thread first emerged. Pull it part way through, so that most of it is above the fabric. Hold the needle eye below the fabric with your left hand.

❶ *Wrapping can be clockwise or anticlockwise. Each produces a different result. Based on historical evidence, most Guimarães bullions were wrapped clockwise. However, a small quantity of historical Guimarães embroideries used anticlockwise wrapping.*

4 Push the wraps to the base of the needle to sit stacked against the fabric, keeping the thread tensioned with your other fingers.

❶ *Ensure all wraps are right next to each other. If there are gaps between, there will be extra thread to span the extra distance between the wraps. When the bullion is pulled through, that extra thread has to go somewhere. The wraps beside absorb the extra thread, making them slightly bigger. For even wraps, make sure there are no gaps in the wraps on the needle.*

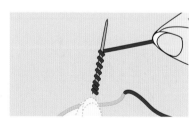

5 Wrap the thread clockwise around the needle a few more times.

❶ *By gently stroking the threads in a clockwise direction the wraps will become tighter. Conversely, stroking in an anticlockwise direction will produce looser wraps, which can be useful when struggling to pull the needle through.*

6 Push the wraps down again. Wrap as many times as are necessary to span the stitch length.

7 Loosely hold the wraps between your thumb and forefinger. Breathe deeply and slowly. Gently and carefully pull the needle through.

❶ *Do not hold the wraps tightly, as it will make it more difficult to pull the needle through.*

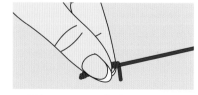

8 When most of the needle and thread is pulled through the wraps, so that the bullion is almost lying against the fabric, then and only then should you release the gentle hold that you have on the wraps.

❶ *When the bullion is almost flat against the fabric, I often put my thumbnail against the end of the bullion's wraps to keep them compact, while continuing to tighten the thread.*

9 Continue to gently pull the thread through the wraps until they lie flat against the fabric.

10 Insert the needle into the fabric at the end of the bullion.

11 Pull the thread through to the back to complete the bullion.

how many wraps?

The number of wraps is determined by the length of the bullion. A long bullion will need more wraps than a short one. By matching the height of the stacked wraps to the stitch length, the number of wraps can be worked out.

If working many bullions of the same length, once you have worked out how many wraps are required for that length, write it on the pattern in pencil, so that you have a note of how many wraps to use.

curved bullions

Curved bullions are worked by adding more wraps than are required for the distance.

For a very curved bullion, add many extra wraps. For a slightly curved bullion, add just a few more.

troubleshooting

lumpy bumpy bullions

Sometimes when pulling the needle through, everything goes haywire and the wraps get all messed up. Do not panic!

1 Before taking the needle to the back, gently pull the thread to pull as much of the extra thread through.

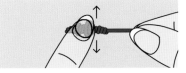

2 At the same time, gently roll your forefinger back and forth across the bullion. This helps the wraps to even out and become smooth.

3 Keep manipulating the bullion until it is as neat as it should be. Finish the bullion as usual.

❶ *Most bullions can be resurrected. Just be persistent.*

bullions with tapered ends

Sometimes bullions are tapered towards one end. This is usually because there are not enough wraps to cover the distance, so the last few have to stretch out to fill it.

To fix this, you will need more wraps to fill the distance. I usually fill my needle with what I judge to be enough wraps to span the length of the bullion, then add one or two more for good measure.

eyelets

Ilhó de rolinho

Eyelets are small bound-edge holes in the fabric. Do not be afraid to tighten the stitches to pull the eyelet open!

1 From the front, take a very short stitch. Pull the thread most of the way through, so there is a tiny tail showing.
❶ *You can also use a small knot and cut it off once the backstitching is done.*

2 Insert the needle between the tail and where the thread emerged, piercing the stitch on the back of the fabric.

3 Bring the needle up a short way around the circle. Insert the needle next to the first stitch, piercing the stitch on the back of the fabric.

4 Work short running stitches, going under only about one fabric thread, and over two or three, so that most of the thread is on the surface.

5 Complete the circle and bring the thread to the front just outside the stitching. Leave the thread hanging from the front.

6 Make a hole in the centre with your needle, wiggling it to make the hole bigger. Take the needle to the back through the hole.

7 Bring the needle up again just outside the running stitch, working in a clockwise direction. Pull the needle through.

8 Pinch the eyelet with your thumb above and forefinger below the fabric. Pull the thread away from it with the other hand, to enlarge the hole.
❶ *Do not be afraid to pull hard.*

9 Insert the needle in the eyelet again.
❶ *Make sure each of the stitches sit next to the previous one. If they overlap or cross, they will create a lump.*

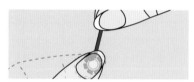

10 Bring the needle out further around the eyelet, just outside the running stitch. Pinch and pull to tighten the stitch.

11 Continue, turning the work. Work the last two stitches loosely, ensuring the needle doesn't catch in them. Bring the thread to the front.

12 On the front, insert the needle in the loops, in an anticlockwise direction. Pull the thread to tighten the loops around the needle.

13 Pull the needle a short way so that the doubled thread sits within the loops. Pull the thread to tighten the loops around the doubled thread.

14 Pull the needle further so that the single thread sits within the loops. Pull the thread to further tighten the loops around the single thread.

15 Pull the thread right through, tightly. Trim the thread.
❶ *If you need to work further stitching around the eyelet, rather than trimming the thread, you can take it to the back.*

16 The completed eyelet.

❶ *If your eyelet hole is very small, you may have tried to cram in too many stitches. You also may not have used strong enough tension when tightening the stitches. Additionally, when tightening, pull away strongly from the eyelet, to open it up.*

buttonholed eyelets
Ilhó de recorte

These eyelets are usually a little larger than regular eyelets. To make the hole bigger, a small cut is made in the fabric in the centre of the eyelet.

1 Take a very short stitch just outside the edge of the guide. Pull the thread nearly all the way through, leaving just a very short tail.

❶ *You can also use a small knot and cut it off once the backstitching is complete.*

2 Insert the needle between the tail and the emerging thread, thereby piercing the stitch on the fabric back.

❶ *If it pulls the thread end through to the back a little more, that is fine. It will probably completely disappear later.*

3 Bring the needle up a little further around the circle. Insert the needle into the backstitch, piercing it.

❶ *This will securely anchor the thread.*

4 Running stitch around the guide with short stitches, going under only a few threads each time, so that most of the thread lies on top of the fabric.

5 Complete the circle and bring the thread to the front just outside the running stitch. Leave the thread hanging from the front.

6 With sharp, fine-pointed scissors make a tiny cut in the centre.

❶ *I usually cut two threads in both directions.*

7 Insert the needle into the hole, holding the thread in a large loop.

8 Bring the needle up inside the large loop. It should emerge from just outside the line of running stitch, a little further around the circle when travelling anticlockwise.

9 Pull the needle through. Tighten by pinching the eyelet (thumb on top and forefinger below), and pulling the thread away from it with the other hand, to enlarge the hole.

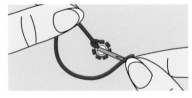

10 Insert the needle into the hole, holding the thread in a large loop.

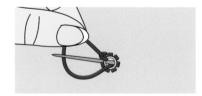

11 Bring the needle up in the large loop. It should emerge just under the running stitch, a little further on from where it last came out, travelling in an anticlockwise direction.

12 Continue around in the same way, pinching and pulling after each stitch to tighten, and to open up the eyelet.

13 To finish, slide the needle toward the centre, under the first stitch, near where it emerged from the fabric.

14 Take the needle to the back through the hole. Run the thread under the back of the stitches to finish.

15 The completed eyelet.

french knot *Nozinho*

French knots are sometimes used scattered, as a filling stitch.

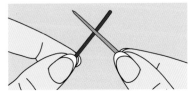

1 Use a straw needle. Bring the thread out of the fabric. Lay the needle on top of the thread.

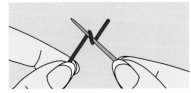

2 Wind the thread around the needle once (or the number of times that are required). Take the needle point back over to where the thread emerges from the fabric.

❶ *More wraps will produce a larger knot.*

3 Insert the needle slightly to the right of the emerging thread (a few fabric threads in between).

❶ *Do not yet take the needle all the way through the fabric.*

❶ *If the needle goes in exactly the same hole, the knot may disappear to the back.*

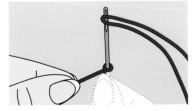

4 Hold the needle point below the fabric with your right hand. Tighten the wrap(s) at the base of the needle, so they sit flush against the fabric, to give a neat, compact knot.

5 Gently pull the needle and thread through to the back of the fabric to complete the finished knot.

herringbone stitch *Espinha*

Herringbone stitch is used to make decorative hems in Guimarães embroidery. The hem is folded to the front, rather than to the back as is usual.

1 Prepare the hem by folding down the raw edge the distance that is required, to the front of the fabric.

2 Folding to the front again, fold down the same amount of fabric as before, to encase the raw edge.

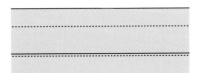

3 Use two guide lines, with the top one along the hem, and the bottom one on the main fabric just next to the hem fold.

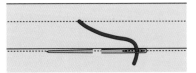

4 Anchor the thread within the hem and bring it out on the top line. A little to the right, take a short stitch from right to left, on the bottom line. Pull the needle through.

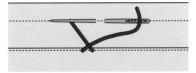

5 Using the same spacing and stitch length as before, take a short stitch under only the top layer of hem fabric from right to left on the top line. Pull the needle through.

6 Using the same spacing and stitch length as before, take a short stitch in the bottom line, from right to left. Pull the needle through.

7 Repeat steps 5 and 6 to build up a line of stitching.

turning a corner

Because herringbone stitch is used around hems, it often needs to turn corners.

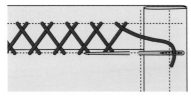 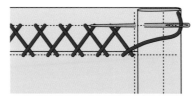 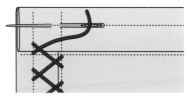

1 Work up to the corner, with a stitch on the lower line right in the corner.
❶ *You may need to adjust the spacing up to the corner to get this to happen.*

2 Pull the needle through. Continuing with the same spacing and stitch length, work a stitch on the upper line.

3 Turn the work 90 degrees anticlockwise. Pull the needle through. Work a stitch in the upper line in a corresponding position to the one on the previous side.

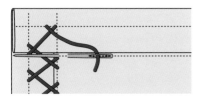 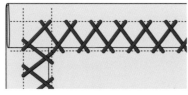

4 Pull the needle through. Using the same spacing and stitch length as before, take a short stitch in the bottom line, from right to left.

5 Continue working in the same manner to build up a line of stitching.

slipping the end into the beginning

When herringbone stitch is worked around an entire article, the end should meet the beginning with a smooth and seamless join.

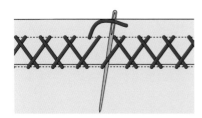  

1 Approach the start of the stitching so that the last stitch will be the same length as the rest. Slide the needle under the first stitch's bottom end.
❶ *You may need to gently adjust the spacing to get this to happen.*

2 Pull the needle through. Using similar spacing as for the other stitches, take the needle through to the back a little to the right of the bottom of the first stitch.

3 Pull the needle through to the back and fasten the thread in the back of the stitching or within the hem.

padded satin stitch

Cheio

This satin stitch has two layers of stitching. The first layer pads the second, giving it a rounded effect with more height than just a single layer.

1 Bring the thread out at the top of the circle guide.

2 Insert the needle at the bottom edge, directly below where the thread emerged.

3 Pull the needle through, so that the stitch sits flat against the fabric. Bring the needle out on the guide, just left of the previous stitch.

4 Insert the needle directly below, on the lower edge of the guide, so that the stitch will be parallel to the first stitch.

❶ *The stitches should be close enough that no fabric is visible between them.*

5 Pull the needle through, so that the stitch sits flat against the fabric. Bring the needle out on the guide, just left of the previous stitch.

❶ *Never work back and forth across the shape. The stitches will curve slightly, and not sit properly.*

6 Insert the needle directly below, on the lower edge of the guide, so that the stitch is parallel to the previous stitch. Pull the needle through so that the stitch sits flat.

❶ *All stitches should be parallel, and the same distance apart.*

7 When the first half of the shape is complete, turn the work 180 degrees. Bring the needle out on the guide, just left of the centre stitch.

8 Insert the needle directly below, on the lower edge of the guide, so that the stitch will be parallel to the first stitch.

9 Complete the satin stitch as for the first half of the shape.

❶ *Starting at the centre and working out to the sides creates neater ends, rather than starting at one side and working across to the other.*

10 Turn the work 90 degrees, and bring the needle out at the top of the circle. The needle should poke out from just underneath the previous stitching.

❶ *This begins the second layer of stitching, where the stitches will sit perpendicular to the padding layer.*

11 Angling the needle so that it goes just underneath the existing stitch at the bottom, insert it at the lower edge.

❶ *This slightly conceals the ends of the stitch, giving a smoother edge to the satin stitch.*

12 Complete the second layer of satin stitch over the first, in the same manner as for the first layer, but slightly concealing the ends of the stitches of the first layer.

❶ *Keep the tension, spacing and angle of the stitches constant throughout.*

sham hem stitch *Formiga*

This stitch is usually used as a decorative line, though can also be used as a hemming stitch, as the name suggests. It is worked in two passes: the first is a counted framework and the second is interlaced on this framework.

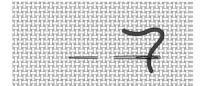

1 Use a tapestry needle. Bring the needle out of the fabric, and then insert it two threads left and six threads down. Bring it out again four threads to the left.

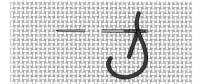

2 Pull the needle and thread through. Insert the needle two threads left and up six from where the thread emerged. Bring it out again four threads to the left.

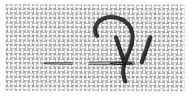

3 Pull the needle and thread through. Insert the needle two threads left and down six from where the thread emerged. Bring it out again four threads to the left.

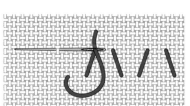

4 Continue stitching the base framework. To complete the first pass and start the second one, bring the needle out one thread on from where it was inserted.

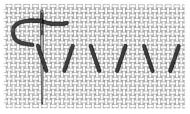

5 Pull the needle and thread through. From above, slide the needle under the last framework stitch.

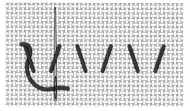

6 From below, slide the needle under the next stitch.

❶ *When pulled through, the stitch should gently curve around and sit over the ends of the framework stitches. If you pull too tight, it will not sit correctly.*

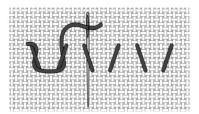

7 Continue sliding the needle under the next stitch, alternating up and down.

❶ *Use gentle tension, so that the interlaced stitches sit over the ends of the framework stitches.*

8 To finish, take the needle to the back one thread further on from the last framework stitch.

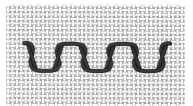

9 The completed sham hem stitch.

stem stitch

Pé-de-flor

1 Use one guide line. Bring the needle out on the line. Insert it a short distance to the right.

2 Pull the needle through. Leave the stitch hanging down. Bring the needle out on the line, above the stitch, and halfway along it.

❶ *Leaving the stitch hanging down out of the way assists with needle placement for beginning the next stitch.*

❶ *Always bring the needle out above the stitching.*

3 Pull the needle through and tighten the thread so that the previous stitch lies flat. Insert the needle a stitch length to the right.

❶ *The stitches half overlap each other.*

4 Pull the needle through but leave the stitch curving down gently. Bring the needle out halfway along the stitch, emerging through the same hole as the end of the first stitch.

❶ *Bring the needle out above the stitch.*

5 Continue in the same way to build up a line of stitching.

wide stem stitch *Pé-de-flor duplo*

1 Use two guide lines, quite close together. Bring the needle out on the top line, then insert it on the lower line, a little way to the right.

2 Pull the needle and thread through. Bring the needle out a little way to the right of the top end of the previous stitch on the top line.

3 Pull the needle and thread through. Moving right the same distance as before, insert the needle in the lower line.

4 Pull the needle and thread through. Using the same spacing as previously, bring the needle out on the top line.

5 Continue working stitches as required.

additional
techniques

damp stretching

The purpose of damp stretching is to make the embroidery as flat as possible, eliminating the need for ironing. The work is dampened, stretched and pinned, then left to dry. It is a technique that is particularly appropriate for whitework embroidery, as there are no colours that will run when it is dampened.

1 Complete the embroidery and remove any tacking. Gently hand wash the embroidery to remove any pencil marks. Remove excess water.

2 Lay the damp embroidery face up on the pinning surface.

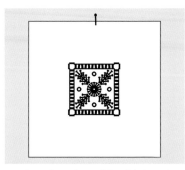

3 Near the edge of the fabric, place a pin in the centre of one side.
❶ *If you are using dressmaking pins, angle the pin slightly so that it leans away from the centre of the embroidery.*

4 Gently pull on the fabric's opposite edge. With the fabric gently stretched, place another pin directly opposite the first one.
❶ *If stretching a piece that has already been hemmed, pin on the stitching line and use lots of pins so that the fabric does not bow or curve between the pins.*

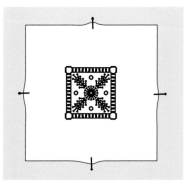

5 Without distorting the grain through the centre of the fabric (e.g. pulling it too far to one side) pin the centre of the other two sides, applying a gentle stretch to the fabric.

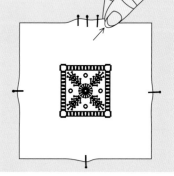

6 Moving outwards a little way to each side of the first pin, stretch away from the centre and from the previous pin, and place the next pins, one on each side.
❶ *The pins may need to be very close to each other or further apart. If the fabric curves or bows between pins, you will need to place the pins closer together.*

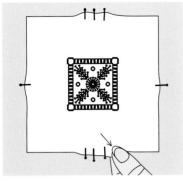

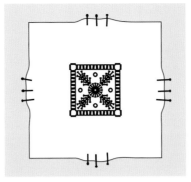

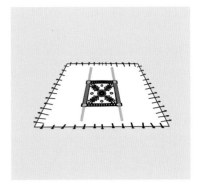

7 Move to the opposite side and repeat the process.

8 Repeat for the other two sides.

❶ *Try to keep tension constant across all the pins, so that the amount of stretch is the same throughout. If you need to, take pins out and restretch sections.*

❶ *Get down low above the surface of the embroidery and look across it. The drawn thread rows should look straight and parallel, like train lines. If they don't, remove the pins in the offending area and retension the fabric.*

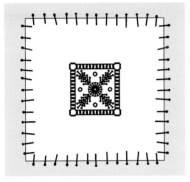

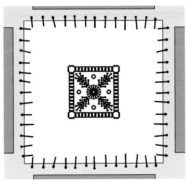

9 Continue similarly, moving out from the centre towards the corners, stretching the fabric away from the centre and the previous pins to stretch out the fabric.

10 When the entire piece is stretched, leave it to dry completely.

❶ *If the edges of the mat you have pinned into curl upwards under the tension of the fabric, place heavy weights (e.g. books, boxes) on the edges of the mat to keep it all flat.*

❶ *The stretching can also be done with dry fabric, and then misted with water spray at the end. However, linen is stronger when it is wet, so it makes sense to take advantage of that strength and stretch it when the fabric is already damp.*

11 After stretching, before it dries, you can also reposition the bullions so that they sit in the way you want them to: straighten any bullions that need straightening, and re-curve any bullions that need to sit curved.

12 When the fabric and embroidery are completely dry, remove the pins.

antique hemstitch

This stitch creates a very pretty hem. If using mitred corners, work them first before hemstitching.

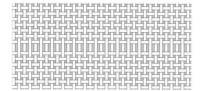

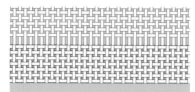

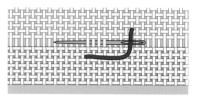

1 Remove one thread across the fabric to create a gap in which to work the decorative hem stitching.

2 On the back of the fabric, create a hem, with the fold meeting the edge of the drawn thread area.

3 Working on the back of the fabric, bring a tapestry needle out two threads away from the gap, within the hem area. Count four threads right, and in the gap, slide the needle under four threads from right to left.
❶ *Any number of threads can be grouped, but three or four is usual.*

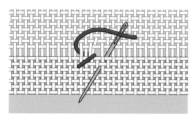

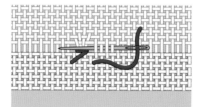

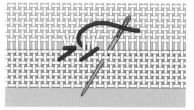

4 Pull the needle through, and gently tighten the stitch. Take the needle under the hem fold where it meets the drawn thread gap. Bring the needle out four threads right of where the thread first emerged.
❶ *The needle goes between the hem and the fabric front, only taking in the hem fabric, so that none of this stitch will be seen on the front.*

5 Pull the needle through and gently tighten the stitch to pull the threads together. Count four threads right, and in the gap, slide the needle under four threads from right to left.

6 Pull the needle through, and gently tighten the stitch. Take the needle under the hem fold, bringing it out four threads right of where the thread previously emerged from within the hem fold.

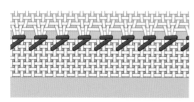

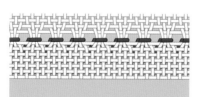

7 Continue in the same way to build up a line of stitching.

❶ *The completed antique hem stitch as seen from the front of the fabric: only the grouping stitches show.*

mitred corners

This method gives a neat mitred corner to hems.

1 With the wrong side of the fabric face up, on one side, fold in the first fold for the hem. Finger press to make a crease.

2 Fold the same amount in again, to encase the raw edge. Press.

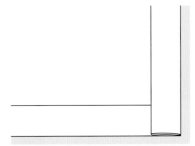

3 On the adjacent side, using the same measurements as for the first side, fold in twice, and press.

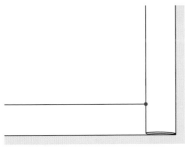

4 Where the two folds meet, mark with a wash-out pencil or HB pencil.

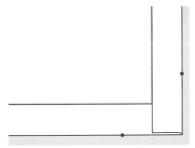

5 Unfold the second fold on each side.

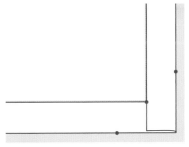

6 Where the two remaining folds meet, mark again.

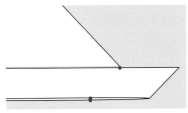

7 With the hems on the outside, fold the fabric diagonally through the corner, matching the dots on the edges of the fabric. Let the extra fabric at the corner unfold.

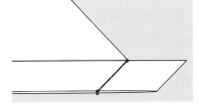

8 Mark a line between the two dots. This is the stitching line. Sew along the line, keeping the first hem folds in place.

❶ *Once the hem corner has been mitred, you can then either hemstitch by hand, or sew the hem by machine.*

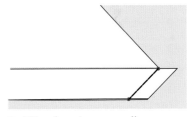

9 Trim the mitre seam allowance to 6 mm (¼ in).

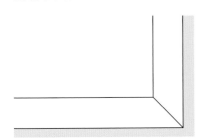

10 Turn the corner the right way out, with the seam open flat and the first hem fold tucked inside the hem.

lacing fabric

This technique can be used to tightly stretch embroidered or plain fabric over a board, to prepare them for finishing. The board can be padded or unpadded.

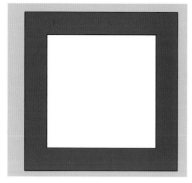

1 Centre the cardboard over the back of the fabric.

❶ *If there is embroidery on the fabric, make sure it is exactly centred.*

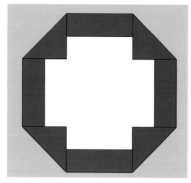

2 Fold the corners of the fabric in over the corners of the cardboard. Finger press.

❶ *Folding in the corners will help to reduce bulk, and give a neater corner.*

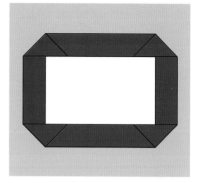

3 Keeping the corners in place, fold down the top and bottom sides.

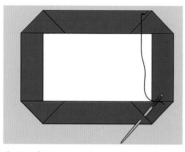

4 With a very long doubled-over thread, start in the top right corner with a few backstitches. Take the needle across to the other side and bring it out through the folded flap.

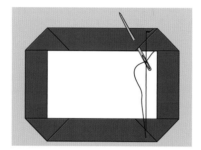

5 Pull the needle and thread through and tighten. Take the needle across to the other side and bring it out through the folded flap.

❶ *The idea is that the thread is very tight, so that the fabric is stretched taut around the board.*

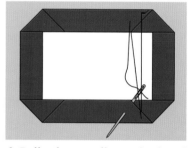

6 Pull the needle and thread through and tighten. Take the needle across to the other side and bring it out through the folded flap.

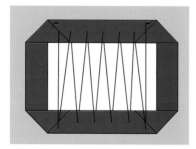

7 Keep working back and forth between the folded flaps, to the other side. Ensure that the thread is very taut before ending off with a few back stitches.

❶ *You can go back to the beginning of the lacing, and pull the threads to tighten them, taking out any slack.*

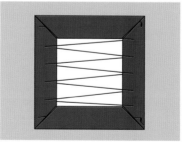

8 Turn the work 90 degrees and fold in the other flaps.

❶ *If you are lacing an embroidery, before this step, turn the work over and check that it is centred. Make any necessary adjustments before continuing.*

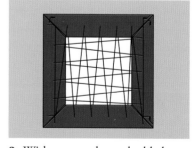

9 With a new long doubled-over thread, lace the second set of flaps tightly.

ladder stitch

Ladder stitch is a simple hand-sewn stitch that can be used to invisibly join together two items, such as the front and back of an ornament, or to close the gap in a pillow seam.

1 Closely align the two edges to be sewn together.

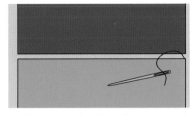

2 Fastening the thread at the back of one of the edges, bring the needle out on that edge at the beginning of the gap to be closed.

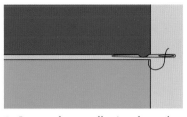

3 Insert the needle in the other edge, directly opposite where the thread emerged, and take a small stitch through the edge.

4 Pull the needle through and gently tighten the stitch a little. Insert the needle in the other edge, directly opposite where the thread emerged, and take a small stitch through the edge.

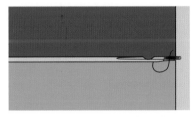

5 Pull the needle through and gently tighten the stitch a little. Insert the needle in the other edge, directly opposite where the thread emerged, and take a small stitch through the edge.

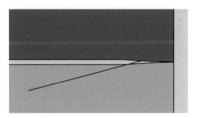

6 After every few stitches, gently pull the thread to bring the edges close together.
❶ *The stitches should disappear between the edges to be almost invisible.*

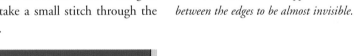

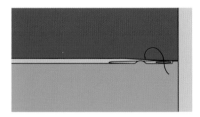

7 Continue stitching from edge to edge.

8 Finish the thread as invisibly as possible with a few neat backstitches in one edge.

index

supplies

Please support your local needlework store by purchasing supplies from them whenever possible. However, if they cannot supply your stitching needs, a full range of Portuguese whitework supplies is available from Vetty Creations.

website www.vettycreations.com.au
email yvette@vettycreations.com.au
postal address
PO Box 1723
Hornsby Westfield NSW 1635
Australia

Left A street in the old town of Guimarães.